PEGGY'S FAVOURITE CAKES & COOKIES

...to make every occasion special

PEGGY PORSCHEN

photographs by Georgia Glynn Smith

Quadrille
PUBLISHING

First published in 2011 by Quadrille Publishing Limited,
Alhambra House, 27–31 Charing Cross Road,
London WC2H OLS

Editorial Director: Jane O'Shea
Creative Director: Helen Lewis
Editor and Project Manager: Lewis Esson
Photography: Georgia Glynn Smith
Designers: Katherine Case, Chalkley Calderwood

Text and designs © Peggy Porschen 2005, 2007, 2011
Photographs © Georgia Glynn Smith 2005, 2007, 2011
Edited text, design and layout © Quadrille Publishing Limited 2005, 2007, 2011

Based on material originally published, in *Cake Chic*, *Pretty Party Cakes*
and *Romantic Cakes*

Cataloguing in Publication Data: a record for this book is available
from the British Library

ISBN 978 1 84400 950 3

Printed and bound in China

Contents

Cookies

Flower Basket Cookies

A friend of mine once asked me for a gift idea for the flower girls at her wedding, so I came up with these flower basket cookies in the colours of the wedding flowers. Delicately wrapped in tissue paper and presented in a lovely gift box as shown overleaf, they also make a perfect little gift for Mother's Day or even just a little token to say 'thank you' to someone.

FOR 6 BASKET COOKIES AND
12 MINI FLOWER COOKIES
6 vanilla cookies (see page 170) in the shape of a basket
12 vanilla circular cookies (see page 170), about 1½ inch (3.75cm) in diameter
12 mini sugar blossoms in each of three colours: pink, purple and white (see pages 195–6)
500g royal icing (see page 191)
food colours (yellow, pink, purple)

EQUIPMENT
bowls
small palette knife
paper piping bags (see page 193)
Wilton piping nozzle 103

TO MAKE THE BASKETS:

1 First mix your colours and prepare your icing bags. You will need 2 piping bags filled with soft-peak icing, one in pastel pink and the other in pastel purple, together with 2 piping bags filled with runny icing in the same colours.

2 Using pink and purple soft-peak icing, pipe the outline of 3 baskets, including the handle, in each colour.

3 Fill in the centre of each cookie with runny icing of the same colour as the outline. Let dry.

4 Stick 6 sugar blossoms (2 of each colour) into the centre of each basket and let them cascade down.

5 Finish the lock by piping little green leaves next to the flowers as shown opposite.

MINI FLOWER COOKIES

TO MAKE THE MINI FLOWER COOKIES:
To make a selection of pink, purple and white flower cookies, follow the same technique as in Royal Iced Flowers on page 195. Use the cookie as you would use the flower nail (without the paper, of course) and pipe the flower directly on it, using nozzle 103 (see 1–2). Once these are dry, snip a 'v'-shape from the tip of a paper piping bag (see 3-4) and use it to pipe little green leaves around the flowers (see 5).

'*a perfect little gift for Mother's Day*'

Birthday Razzle Dazzle

Decorating cookies is one of my favourite things to do as it is actually a lot easier than it looks. Create your own style, but keep your cookies smart and simple. Colourful patterns of dots and stripes piped on a plain background make very effective designs. You can either use them as a treat for guests at your own party – for instance, they make excellent place cards with guests' names written on them – or take them as gifts to a birthday party, presented stylishly gift-wrapped.

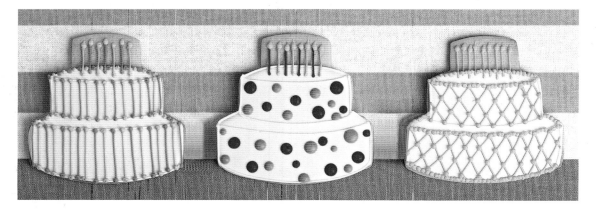

FOR ABOUT 10–12 COOKIES
10–12 cookies (see page 170) shaped as gift boxes and cakes about 400g royal icing (see page 191) selection of food colours

EQUIPMENT
small palette knife
paper piping bags (see page 193)

FOR THE GIFT BOXES
1 First spread on the background colour: fill 1 piping bag with soft-peak royal icing and 1 with runny.

2 Using soft-peak icing, pipe the outline of the box and let set

briefly. Then, with a bag of runny icing, fill in the centre of the box. Leave to dry for at least half an hour. Repeat with the remaining cookies and icing.

3 Choose a colour for the bow and fill one piping bag with soft-peak and one with runny icing in that colour. Pipe the outline and, once that sets, fill in the centre. Let dry.

4 Once the icing is completely dry, pipe the outline and the lines marking the individual sections once more to create a 3-D look. for the birthday cakes

FOR THE BIRTHDAY CAKES
5 Again, start with a background colour (white this time). Pipe the outline in soft-peak icing. Once set, fill in the centre with runny icing and let dry. Pipe the outline and the lines marking 'tiers' again.

6 Choose colours and decoration and prepare piping bags. For stripes, use soft-peak icing; for dots, thin down soft-peak icing with a little water to make it slightly runny.

7 Decorate the 'sides' with stripes or dots. Pipe candles on the 'top' with yellow icing for flames.

Baby Shower

What a quite perfect – and very personal gift – these will make for your best friend's baby shower. Wrap your selection of cute baby-themed cookies in an attractive presentation tin or box lined with tissue paper and tie it with a beautiful matching satin ribbon. If you already know the baby's name, why not pipe it on top of one of the cookies? If you don't know whether the baby is a girl or a boy, just make a mix of pink, blue and yellow iced cookies.

FOR 8 COOKIES
8 vanilla cookies (see page 170) in the shapes of a building block, a baby's bib, a pram, a baby's bottle, a baby sleep suit, 2 bootees and a rattle,
300g royal icing (see page 191)
food colours (pink, baby blue, yellow)

EQUIPMENT
bowls
small palette knife
paper piping bags (see page 193)

First prepare your colours and piping bags. You will need 1 bag of soft-peak icing in each colour, 2 piping bags of runny white, 1 of runny blue icing and 1 small bag of runny yellow icing.

TO MAKE THE BUILDING BLOCK:
1 Using white soft-peak icing, pipe a white outline.

2 Using runny white icing, fill in the centre and let dry.

3 Using the blue soft-peak icing, pipe the outline again and the sides of the block, as well as the outlines for the alphabet letters.

4 Using runny blue icing, fill in the centres of the alphabet letters and let dry.

TO MAKE THE BABY'S BIB:
1 Using blue soft-peak icing, pipe the outline for the bow.

2 Using white soft-peak icing, pipe the outline for the bib.

3 Using blue runny icing, fill in the centre of the bow. Let dry.

4 Using white runny icing, fill in the centre of the bib. Let dry.

5 Using blue soft-peak icing, pipe the lines of the bow.

6 Using white soft-peak icing, pipe the outline of the bib again. Let dry.

TO MAKE THE PRAM:

1 Using white soft-peak icing, pipe the outline of the hood.

2 Using blue soft-peak icing, pipe the outline of the rest of the pram.

3 Using white runny icing, fill in the centre of the hood.

4 Using blue runny icing, pipe the outline of the rest of the pram. Let dry.

5 Using white soft-peak icing, pipe the outlines again, and the wheels, as well as adding some detail to the pram hood. Let dry.

TO MAKE THE BABY'S BOTTLE:

1 Using white soft-peak icing, pipe the outline for the bottle.

2 Using blue soft-peak icing, pipe the outline for the top in blue.

3 Using yellow soft-peak icing, pipe the outline for the dummy. Let dry.

4 Fill in the centres with runny icing using the same colours. Let dry.

5 Pipe the outlines of the individual parts again using the same icing as before.

6 Using white soft-peak icing, pipe a millilitre scale on the front of the bottle. Let dry.

TO MAKE THE BABY SLEEP SUIT:
Follow the same procedure as for the bootees (above right), piping the outline first, then fill in the centre and pipe the dots. Finish by repeating the outline and piping some details of the suit.

TO MAKE THE BOOTEES

1 Using white soft-peak icing, pipe the outlines for the bootees.

2 Using white runny icing, fill in the centres.

3 While that is still wet, use blue runny icing to pipe small dots all over the bootees, so that they level out with the white icing. Let everything dry.

4 Using blue soft-peak icing, pipe the blue ribbon bow.

6 Using white soft-peak icing, pipe the outline of the bootees again. Let dry.

TO MAKE THE RATTLE:
Follow the same procedure as for the bootees, piping the outline first, then fill in the centres and pipe the dots for the bow. Finish by repeating the outlines and details of the bow.

Butterfly Cookies

The challenge is to find the butterflies... this is just one of many examples of how an attractive piece of printed fabric can instantly inspire you into creating something simply gorgeous, like these brilliant little butterflies. Use these for a summer tea party or picnic lunch.

FOR ABOUT 10 COOKIES:
choice of food colour
   (here pastel pink)
300g royal icing (see page 191)
10 vanilla cookies in butterfly
   shape (see page 170)

EQUIPMENT
bowls
small palette knife
paper piping bags (see page 193)

1 Prepare 1 piping bag of white soft-peak icing for the outline and the body, and one piping bag of runny pastel-pink icing for filling in the centre. For piping the little dots, thin down bright pink soft-peak icing with a little water to make it slightly runny and put in a third bag.

2 Start by piping the white outline of the wings.

3 Once the outlines are set, fill in the wing centres with the pastel-pink icing. Let these dry for about half an hour.

4 Once the wings have dried, snip the tip of the piping bag containing the white icing to make it slightly larger and pipe the body between the wings, starting from the top and pulling it down towards you.

5 Finally, pipe little dots all over the wings, using your bright pink runny icing.

Cookie Catwalk

As if they have just come from the latest fashion shows in Paris or Milan, you can create your own cookie catwalk to reflect the season's latest trends and colours, using nothing more than the tip of a piping bag and some appropriately coloured icing.

FOR 12 COOKIES
12 chocolate cookies (see page 170) in the shape of handbags, dresses and shoes
500g royal icing (see page 191)
food colours (chocolate-brown, pink)

EQUIPMENT
bowl
small palette knife
paper piping bags (see page 193)

First prepare your colours and piping bags. You will need 1 bag of soft-peak icing in each colour and 3–4 piping bags of runny icing in each colour.

TO MAKE THE HANDBAGS:
1 Using soft-peak icing in your colour of choice, pipe the outline of the body of the handbag.

2 Fill in the centre with runny icing of the same colour as for the outline. Let dry.

3 Using soft-peak icing of a different colour, repeat the piping of the outline and add details like a bow and the handbag handle. Let dry.

TO MAKE THE SHOES:
1 Using soft-peak icing in your colour of choice, pipe the outline of the shoe.

2 Fill in the centre with runny icing of the same colour as the outline. Let dry.

3 Using soft-peak icing of the same colour, repeat the outline and add details like a bow or a dot design. For dot designs, pipe dots into the still-soft icing (see Baby Bootees, page 16); for bows, wait until the basic colour underneath has set.

TO MAKE THE DRESSES:
1 For full dresses outline, fill in and decorate the cookies using the same techniques as above.

2 For 2-piece outfits, outline the top and the skirt separately using soft-peak icing in two different colours.

3 Fill in the top first and let dry. Then fill in the skirt and let that dry.

4 Repeat the outlining of the cookies using the same icing, and add small details like collars, belts or bows. Let dry.

5 For dot designs, pipe dots into the still-soft icing (see Baby Bootees, page 16); for collars, belts or bows, wait until the basic colour underneath has set.

Snowflake Cookies

These sparkly little jewels are easy to make and will add a magical touch to any Christmas party. To turn them into strikingly original tree ornaments, simply poke a hole into the cookies before you bake them and then hang them up using lengths of satin ribbon.

FOR 6 COOKIES
300g royal icing (see page 191)
6 gingerbread cookies (see page 171) shaped as snowflakes
white edible glitter

EQUIPMENT
bowls
small palette knife
paper piping bags (see page 193)

1 First prepare your icing bags. Fill 1 with white soft-peak icing and 2 with white runny icing.

2 Pipe the outline of the cookie, including the design in the centre.

3 Using white runny icing, fill in the centre.

4 While still wet, drizzle white glitter generously over the icing until completely covered. Let dry.

5 Before use, shake off any excess glitter.

Bride and Groom Cookies

Use these as wedding favours or as a token to accompany your gift. To add a personal touch, match the designs to the real wedding gowns.

FOR 3 BRIDE AND 3 GROOM COOKIES
about 600g royal icing
    (see page 191)
black food colour
3 cookies made in the shape of
    prom dresses (about
    12.5x10cm/5x4 inches) and 3
    in the shape of tuxedos (about
    7.5x11cm/3x4½ inches) made
    using 1 recipe quantity of
    sugar cookie dough
    (see page 170)

EQUIPMENT
2 small bowls
small palette knife
paper piping bags (see page 193)
pair of scissors
cling film or a damp cloth

1 Divide the icing between two bowls, about 250g in one and 350g in the other. Mix the 250g with black food colour. Add a little water to both bowls until the icings have reached soft-peak consistency (see page 192). Fill one piping bag with each colour.

2 Snip a small tip off the bag with black icing and pipe the outline of each groom in a steady smooth line (see 1 and page 194). Do the same with the white icing on the bride cookies. Cover the bags with cling film or damp cloth to prevent the icing drying out.

3 Dilute the remaining white and black icing with a few drops of water to a runny consistency (see page 192). Fill one piping bag with each colour and flood the centres of the cookies in the appropriate colours, being careful not to overflow the sides. Flood the tuxedo centres with white first (see 2), let dry and then flood the black part (see 3).

4 Once dry, pipe the detail on each cookie, using the soft-peak icing (see 4). Let dry.

1   2   3   4

Heart-shaped Place Cards

This clever idea turns a simple heart cookie into a stunning decorative feature at the dinner table. You can use other cookie shapes as well, as long as they provide enough space for writing names on the top. If you find using the ribbon too fiddly, you can wrap each heart in a cellophane bag and place it on top of each dinner plate. This way your guests can take the cookie home as a personalised keepsake.

FOR 10 COOKIES

10 cookies made in heart shapes (about 6cm/2½ inches) using ½ recipe quantity of sugar cookie dough (see page 170)
350g royal icing (see page 191)
dusky-pink and dark-brown food colours (Sugarflair)

EQUIPMENT

small round cutter
small bowl
small palette knife
paper piping bags (see page 193)
pair of scissors
cling film or damp cloth
1.25m pastel-pink ribbon, 15 mm width

1 As soon as the heart cookies come out of the oven, cut a little hole at the top of each, using the small round cutter. Be careful as the tray will be hot. Let them cool down.

2 Once the cookies are cold, start with the brown outline. In a bowl, mix about 300g icing with a small amount of brown colour. Add a little water until it has reached soft-peak consistency (see page 192). Put some of the icing into a piping bag. Snip a small tip off the piping bag and pipe around the outlines of the hearts (see page 194).

3 Should you have any icing left over in the bag, squeeze it back into the bowl with the remaining brown icing and dilute it with a few drops of water to a runny consistency (see page 192). Put this into a fresh piping bag. Again, snip the tip off and fill the centre of the cookies with the runny icing, being careful not to overflow the sides. Let dry.

4 Once dry, mix the remaining royal icing with dusky-pink food colour and a little water to soft-peak consistency. Put it into a piping bag, snip off a small tip and pipe a squiggly outline around the sides of the hearts. Pipe names or initials in the centre. Let dry.

5 Once completely dry (ideally leave overnight), push a piece of ribbon through the hole and tie into a knot or a bow. Attach to a champagne glass or a napkin as a place card.

Rosebud Cookies

To complement the rosebud design, I have scented the icing with rosewater. Wrapped in a pretty gift box or cellophane bags, these gorgeous little cookies make an exquisite gift or wedding favour.

FOR ABOUT 12 COOKIES
about 450g royal icing
   (see page 191)
red, pink and green food colours
small amount of rosewater
12 cookies in the shape of
   rosebuds, made from 1 recipe
   quantity of vanilla sugar
   cookie dough (see page 170)

EQUIPMENT
several small bowls
small palette knife
few paper piping bags
   (see page 193)
pair of scissors
cling film or a damp cloth

1 Place about 300g of royal icing in a bowl and colour it with red food colour. Add a few drops of rosewater until the icing has reached soft-peak consistency (see page 192). Put a small amount in a piping bag.

2 Snip a small tip off the piping bag and pipe the outlines for the flowering top of the buds on the cookies, leaving enough space for the green leaves at the bottom of the cookies. Pipe all the red outlines first.

3 Should you have any red icing left over in the bag, squeeze it back into the bowl with the remaining red icing and dilute it with a few drops of rosewater to a runny consistency (see page 192). Put this in a fresh piping bag. Again, snip a tip off the piping bag and fill the red-outline centres of the bud heads with the runny icing, being careful not to overflow the sides. Let dry before piping on the green stems.

4 Once the red icing has dried completely, take about 100g of icing and colour it green. Put a small amount in a piping bag, pipe the outline of the stems first, then, as in step 3, make some runny green icing and flood the centres with that and fill the centres of the stems. Let dry. Reserve a small amount of soft-peak green icing to trace the outline of the stems and leaves later.

5 Mix the remaining 50g of icing with pink food colour and trace the individual petals of the rosebuds. Let dry.

6 Once dry, trace the outline of the stems using the reserved green icing. Let dry.

Wedding Cake Cookies

This idea gives you the option of coordinating the design of your wedding favour with your wedding cake, making a lovely memento for your guests to take home or to send to those who were unable to make it – if they live overseas, for example.

FOR 6 COOKIES
600g royal icing (see page 191)
baby-blue food colour
6 cookies in the shape of
    wedding cakes (about
    10x12.5cm/4x5 inches),
    made using 1 recipe quantity
    of sugar cookie dough,
    (see page 170)

EQUIPMENT
small bowl
small palette knife
paper piping bags (see page 193)
pair of scissors
cling film or damp cloth

1 In a small bowl, mix about 450g of royal icing with a little water to soft-peak consistency (see page 192). Put some of the icing into a piping bag.

2 Snip a small tip off the piping bag and pipe the outline of the cake shape for each cookie in a steady smooth line (see page 194). Cover the piping bag with the leftover icing with cling film or a damp cloth to prevent it drying out.

3 Dilute the remaining icing with a few drops of water to a runny consistency (see page 192). Put it in a piping bag and flood the centres of the cookies, being careful not to overflow the sides. Let dry.

4 Once dry, mix 150g of icing with a little blue food colour and a small amount of water to give a soft-peak consistency (see page

192). Pipe the outline of the bow detail on each cookie. Cover the piping bag with any leftover icing with cling film or a damp cloth to prevent it drying out.

5 Dilute the remaining blue icing with a small amount of water to a runny consistency (see page 192), put it in a piping bag and use to flood the centre of the bow. Let dry.

6 With the remaining soft-peak white icing, pipe the outline for the individual cake tiers and a dotted border at the bottom. With the remaining soft-peak blue icing, pipe the detail of the bow. Let dry.

Risqué Lingerie

Make little goody bags filled with these cookies for a hen night. If you're already married, make them for your valentine or husband to give him a taste of what is in store for later.

FOR ABOUT 4 ONE-PIECE LINGERIE COOKIES AND 4 TWO-PIECE COOKIES
600g royal icing (see page 191)
pink and red food colours
4 cookies in the shape of a one-piece swim suit (about 6x10cm/2½x4 inches) and 4 cookies each in the shape of bras and knickers (about 7.5cm/3 inch square), made using 1 recipe quantity of sugar or gingerbread cookie dough (see pages 170–1)

EQUIPMENT
3 small bowls
small palette knife
paper piping bags (see page 193)
pair of scissors
cling film or a damp cloth

1 Divide the royal icing equally between 3 small bowls. Colour one with pink and one with red food colour, and keep the third one white. Add a small amount of water to each until the icing has reached soft-peak consistency (see page 192). Put a small amount of each colour into a piping bag and keep the remaining icing covered with cling film or a damp cloth to prevent it drying out.

2 Snip a small tip off each bag and pipe the outlines for the bras, the knickers and the camisoles for each cookie (see 1). Keep the piping bags covered with cling film to prevent the icing from drying out.

3 Dilute the icing remaining in the bowls with a small amount of water to a runny consistency (see page 192) and put into 3 fresh piping bags. Flood the centres of each cookie with the same colour as the outline, then use a different colour to pipe little dots on the still-wet base (see 2). This way the dots will sink in and form a smooth surface with the main icing. Let dry.

4 Once everything is dry, pipe the details, i.e. the frills, straps and little bows, using the reserved soft-peak icing (see 3). Let dry.

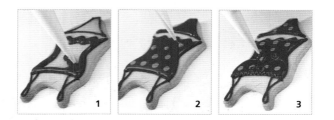

Tea For Two

These funky retro-inspired teapots and teacups will make the perfect addition to any tea party or a bridal party.

❀ ❀ ❀ ❀ ❀ ❀ ❀ ❀ ❀ ❀ ❀ ❀ ❀ ❀ ❀ ❀ ❀ ❀ ❀ ❀

FOR 4 TEAPOT AND 4 TEACUP COOKIES
about 600g royal icing
   (see page 191)
pink, blue and green food
   colours
4 cookies in the shape of teapots
   (about 7.5x10cm/3x4 inch)
   and 4 in the shape of teacups
   (about 7.5x8.5cm/3x3½
   inches), made using 1 recipe
   quantity of sugar cookie
   dough (see page 170)

EQUIPMENT
3 small bowls
small palette knife
paper piping bags (see page 193)
pair of scissors
cling film or a damp cloth

1 Divide the royal icing equally between 3 bowls. Mix one amount of icing with pink and one with blue food colour, and keep the other one white. Add a little water to all three until they have reached soft-peak consistency (see page 192). Fill one piping bag with each colour.

2 One at a time, snip a small tip off each piping bag and pipe the outline of each cookie in a steady smooth line (see page 194), decorating one cup and one teapot in each colour. Cover the piping bags with cling film or a damp cloth to prevent the icing drying out.

3 Dilute each of the remaining bowls of icing with a few drops of water to a runny consistency (see page 192). Fill one piping bag with each colour and flood the centres of the appropriately coloured cookies, being careful not to overflow the sides.

4 Once they are dry, pipe the outlines, including the lids and handles, using a contrasting colour (white on pink or blue on white), using the soft-peak icing.

5 Using the soft-peak icing, pipe different designs on each cookie, such as polka dots, stripes, hearts and little rosebuds. For the little leaves of the rosebuds, mix some leftover white icing with green food colour, snip the tip of the piping bag in a V shape and pipe the leaves. Let dry.

Mini Heart Favours

For obvious reasons, iced heart-shaped cookies are among the most popular choices for wedding favours. What makes this particular version so pretty is wrapping the three different shades of pink together in a bag. This idea works for any colour scheme. Instead of using them as favours, you can serve them individually as petits fours, arranged on a cake stand or at the side of a coffee cup.

FOR 24 COOKIES

about 300g royal icing
  (see page 191)
pink food colour
24 cookies in small heart shapes
  (about 3.5cm/1½ inch), made
  using ½ recipe quantity of
  sugar cookie dough
  (see page 170)

EQUIPMENT

small bowl
small palette knife
paper piping bags (see page 193)
pair of scissors
cling film or damp cloth
8 cellophane bags (optional)
about 4m pink satin ribbon
  (optional)

1 Start with the lightest shade of pink. In a bowl, mix one-third of the royal icing with a tiny drop of pink food colour to give a pastel-pink shade. Add a little water until the icing is soft-peak consistency (see page 192). Put some of the icing into a piping bag. Keep the bowl covered.

2 Snip a small tip off the piping bag and pipe the outline of the heart in a steady smooth line (see page 194). Outline 8 of the hearts with the pastel-pink icing.

3 Should you have any icing left over in the bag, squeeze it back into the bowl with the remaining pastel-pink icing and dilute it with a few drops of water to a runny consistency (see page 192). Fill a fresh piping bag with this.

4 Again snip off the tip and fill the centre of the hearts with the runny icing, being careful not to overflow the sides.

5 Repeat steps 1 to 4, using 2 darker shades of pink icing, so you have 8 cookies in each shade.

6 If you like, you can pack 1 of each shade of cookie in a cellophane bag and tie this up decoratively with ribbon.

Cup Cakes

Cup Cake Garden

As the name might suggest, these cup cakes may be decorated with any kind of flower you choose. Make a variety of the sugar flowers as shown on pages 195-6 (here we've used the simple 5-petal flowers only) and place one on each cake. For an attractive and original table centrepiece, you can easily arrange some of these cakes on a pretty cake stand and then bedeck them with some fresh flowers from your garden – or the florist.

FOR 25 CUP CAKES

25 pink 5-petal sugar blossoms (see page 195–6)

25 chocolate cup cakes (made using 1 recipe quantity basic Victoria sponge, see page 174, baked in silver paper cases)

150ml plain sugar syrup (see page 178)

250g chocolate ganache (see page 180)

100g royal icing (see page 191)

green food colour

EQUIPMENT

pastry brush

small palette knife

paper piping bag (see page 193)

scissors

1 Make the sugar blossoms a day in advance, as described on pages 195-6.

2 Using a pastry brush, soak the tops of the cup cakes with the sugar syrup.

3 Using a small palette knife, ice the cup cakes with chocolate ganache. Let set.

4 Place one sugar blossom on top of each cup cake, fixing in place with a little drop of ganache.

5 Mix the royal icing with some green food colour and put it in the piping bag. Cut a 'V' shape in the tip of the bag and pipe some leaves around the flower (see Flower Basket Cookies, page 8).

Daisy Dot Cup Cakes

The decoration of sweet daisies, looking so pure and innocent, makes these pretty cup cakes ideal for celebrating name days or a little girl's birthday party, but they can also serve as adorable treats for people of all types and ages – especially keen gardeners.

FOR 12 CUPCAKES:

MAKE THE SUGAR DAISIES AT LEAST ONE DAY AHEAD

200g white flower paste
   (Squires Kitchen is best)
a little white vegetable fat
icing sugar, for dusting
yellow food colour
caster sugar, for dipping
a little royal icing (see page 191)
12 vanilla cup cakes, iced with
   fondant icing (see pages
   188–190) in pastel colours

EQUIPMENT

small plastic board
PME daisy cutter
small palette knife
foam pad
Cel Stick or toothpick
painter's palette
small rolling pin
artist's brush
paper piping bag (see page 193)

1 Knead the paste with a little vegetable fat until smooth and pliable.

2 Roll out a walnut-sized piece of paste on a plastic board until very thin. Should it want to stick to the board, grease it lightly with the fat.

3 Press the daisy cutter firmly on the paste and cut out the shape (see 1). Carefully lift with a palette knife and lay on the foam pad.

4 Roll the Cel Stick gently back and forth over each petal as shown to shape it (see 2).

5 Dust a painter's palette with icing sugar and place the flower over one of the wells. Push the

centre down gently with the end of the rolling pin (see 3).

6 Mix a small bead of flower paste with a knife tip of yellow food colour and shape to a ball. Brush lightly with water and dip in sugar. Stick in the centre of the daisy with a little water. Repeat to make 12 daisies. Let dry overnight.

DECORATE THE CUP CAKES:

7 Pipe a dot of royal icing on top of each cup cake and stick a daisy on it.

8 Finish by piping little dots of white icing all over the tops.

Kaleidoscope Cakes

My best 'cake mate', Anne Schultes, from Cologne in Germany, gave me this idea. She is one of the most creative, talented and inspiring cake decorators I know and she has been a great support to me throughout my career. Some time ago we decided to adopt a joint motto 'Born to bake and decorate!'. As these cakes are very graphic and their geometric designs are straightforward – however dazzling – they have proved particularly popular with male recipients, so they will make great birthday cup cakes for the man in your life.

FOR 25 CUP CAKES

25 (vanilla or lemon) cup cakes
   (made using 1 recipe quantity
basic Victoria sponge, see
   page 174, baked in silver
   paper cases)
150ml flavoured sugar syrup
   (see page 178)
100g sieved apricot jam
1.5 kg fondant icing
   (see page 188)
selection of food colours
300g royal icing (see page 191)

EQUIPMENT

pastry brush
small saucepan
small palette knife
bowls
paper piping bags (see page 193)
scissors

1 Using a pastry brush, soak the tops of the cup cakes with the sugar syrup.

2 Bring the jam to the boil in a small pan and brush a thin layer on top of each soaked cup cake, using the pastry brush.

3 Make up some fondant icing in different colours and dip the cup cakes in them, as described on page 190. Let dry.

4 Fill your piping bag with soft-peak royal icing, coloured to your choice. Pipe geometrical lines and patterns on top of the cup cakes as shown (also see the basic piping techniques on page 194).

5 Always pipe one colour first on all your cup cakes and let that dry before you pipe the next pattern in a different colour on top.

Bollywood Kitsch Cakes

As the name suggests, the idea for these cakes came to me when Bollywood turned into high fashion and Andrew Lloyd Webber's glittering musical Bombay Dreams premiered, inspiring me to make these sparkling edible jewels.

FOR ABOUT 30 FONDANT FANCIES

30 fondant fancies (made as described on pages 188–9, using 2 recipe quantities basic Victoria sponge and bright pink, yellow, orange, turquoise and purple fondant icing)

15 small pink marzipan roses (see pages 142–143)

45 small pink marzipan rosebuds (see pages 142–143)

90 small green marzipan rose leaves (see page 199)

pink and green edible glitter

100g soft-peak royal icing (see page 191)

edible gold lustre

1 tablespoon clear alcohol (such as vodka)

EQUIPMENT

about 30 golden paper cases

small palette knife

paper piping bags (see page 193)

scissors

fine artist's brush

1 Put the fondant fancies in golden paper cases.

2 Make the roses, rosebuds and leaves as described on pages 142–143. While the marzipan is still wet, dip the flowers in the pink glitter and the leaves in the green.

3 Put the soft-peak royal icing into a paper piping bag and pipe fine swirls or dots on top of the fondant fancies as shown (see 1). Let dry.

4 Mix some gold lustre to a paste with a drop of clear alcohol and use the paintbrush to colour the swirls and dots with it (see 2).

5 Stick the roses and leaves into the middle of each cake using a dab of royal icing (see 3).

Ruffle Rose Cup Cakes

I saw this gorgeously girly cakestand in a department store while I was on a trip to New York, and I just had to have it. Here its romantic ruffle design provides the perfect setting for my wild rose cup cakes, which were inspired by it.

FOR ABOUT 25 CUP CAKES
25 vanilla cup cakes (made using
   1 recipe quantity basic
   Victoria sponge, see page 174,
   baked in white paper cases)
150ml vanilla sugar syrup
   (see page 178)
500g vanilla buttercream
   (see page 179)
75 small dusky pink marzipan
   roses (3 per cup cake,
   see pages 142–143)
150 small moss-green marzipan
   leaves (6 per cup cake,
   see page 199)

EQUIPMENT
pastry brush
small palette knife

1 Using the pastry brush, soak the tops of the cup cakes with the sugar syrup.

2 Using the palette knife, cover the tops with the buttercream.

3 Place the roses and the leaves on top of the cakes, pressing them slightly into the buttercream to fix them in place.

4 Ideally, arrange them on a beautiful old-fashioned cakestand.

Butterfly Fancies

If you want to add a real touch of magic to your party, you can't go wrong with these delicate butterfly fancies. Don't they just look as if they want to fly away? Be careful, though, you'd better keep an eye on them…Perhaps it would be better to eat them first.

FOR ABOUT 25 FANCIES
small amount of vegetable fat
food colours (pink, orange,
    yellow and blue)
350g royal icing (see page 191)
25 small fondant fancies, 4cm/
    1½ inch square (made as
    described on pages 188–9
    – you will need about 1
    (40 x 30/16 x 12 inch) sheet
    of basic Victoria sponge –
    using fondant icing in several
    different candy colours)

EQUIPMENT
sheet of cellophane
butterfly templates
    (see page 206–7)
paper piping bags (see page 193)
thin cardboard
greaseproof paper
scissors
small palette knife
25 silver cup cases

Prepare the butterflies at least 2 days in advance. Place the cellophane on top of the butterfly templates and rub a very thin layer of vegetable fat on top with your hands to prevent the icing sticking.

TO MAKE THE YELLOW BUTTERFLY:
1 Mix your colours and prepare your piping bags. You will need 1 piping bag filled with soft-peak yellow icing, another with soft-peak pale-blue icing, and a third with runny yellow icing.

2 Using the soft-peak yellow icing, pipe the outline of the butterfly.

3 Using the runny yellow icing, fill the top wings and let them dry.

4 Using the same icing, fill the bottom wings and let dry.

5 Using soft-peak pale-blue icing, pipe the little blue dots on top as shown.

TO MAKE THE BLUE BUTTERFLY:
1 Mix your colours and prepare your piping bags. You will need 1 bag filled with soft-peak blue icing, another with soft-peak green (yellow plus blue) icing, and a third with runny blue icing.

2 Using the soft-peak blue icing, pipe the outline of the butterfly.

3 Using the runny blue icing, fill the top wings and let them dry.

4 Using the same icing, fill the bottom wings and let dry.

5 Using soft-peak blue icing, pipe the little blue dots on top as shown.

TO MAKE THE GREEN BUTTERFLY:
1 Mix your colours and prepare your icing bags. You will need 1 piping bag filled with soft-peak bright-green icing, another with runny bright-green icing and a third with runny light-green icing.

2 Using the soft-peak bright-green icing, pipe the outline of the butterfly.

3 Using the runny bright-green icing, fill the top wings and let them dry.

4 Using the runny light-green icing, fill the bottom wings and let dry.

1

2

TO MAKE THE PINK BUTTERFLY:

1 Mix your colours and prepare your icing bags. You will need 1 piping bag filled with soft-peak pale-pink icing, another with runny pale-pink icing and a third with runny bright-pink icing.

2 Using the pale-pink soft-peak icing, pipe the outline of the butterfly.

3 Using the same icing, pipe a parallel line just inside the wing outline, leaving a small border.

4 Using the runny pale-pink icing, fill the gap between these outlines.

5 Using the runny bright-pink icing, fill the centres. Let dry.

TO MAKE THE ORANGE BUTTERFLY:

1 Mix your colours and prepare your icing bags. You will need 1 piping bag filled with soft-peak yellow icing, another with runny yellow icing and a third with runny orange icing.

2 Using the yellow soft-peak icing, pipe the outline of the butterfly.

3 Using the same icing, pipe an inner line as shown outline, leaving a border.

4 Using the runny orange icing, fill the main centres of the wings. Let dry.

5 Using the runny yellow icing, fill the outside border and making the dots. Let dry.

TO FINISH ALL THE BUTTERFLIES:

1 Pipe a couple of feelers for each butterfly in a matching colour on a piece of greaseproof paper.

2 Let everything dry and set for at least 2 days in a warm dry place.

3 Fold some pieces of thin cardboard to a 'V' shape to support the wings when sticking them together and line with a piece of folded greaseproof paper (see 1).

4 Pipe a small line of royal icing in a colour matching the butterfly into the fold of the paper (see 2). Lift the wings with the small palette knife and place them in position on either side of the 'V' shape (see 3). Let the butterflies dry in position for at least 3 hours.

5 Put the fondant fancies in silver cup cases and stick a butterfly on top of each with a dot of stiff-peak royal icing (see 4 and 5).

6 Using soft-peak icing in appropriate colours, pipe a head and a body in the middle between the wings (see 6) and stick two feelers carefully into the head (see 7).

4

5

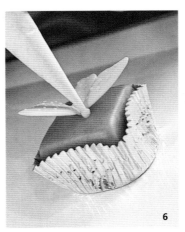
6

7

Je T'Aime Mon Amour...

This simple presentation of little alphabet cakes makes a uniquely personal gift. You can ice any message in this way, or even make it more intriguing by arranging the letters randomly as a kind of puzzle, letting the recipient put the message together.

FOR A MESSAGE LIKE THIS ONE, OF ABOUT 15 LETTERS

about 15 fondant fancies made and dipped as described on pages 188–9, using a 15cm (6-inch) square Victoria sponge (1 recipe quantity, see page 174) and red fondant icing

about 250g royal icing

pink and red food colours

EQUIPMENT

about 15 round silver metallic muffin cases (they don't make square ones, but these mould to shape)

small bowl

small palette knife

paper piping bags (see page 193)

pair of scissors

gift box, wrapping paper and ribbon (optional)

1 Place the fondant fancies into the silver muffin cases. Only round muffin cases are usually available, so you need to shape them round the fondant fancies (see page 188).

2 Place about 200g of royal icing in a small bowl. Using a small palette knife, mix it with pink food colour and a few drops of water until at soft-peak consistency (see page 192). Fill a piping bag with some of the icing and keep the remainder in the covered bowl.

3 Snip the tip off the piping bag and pipe the outlines of the letters on the fondant fancies.

4 If you have any icing left inside the bag, squeeze it back into the bowl and dilute the icing with water, this time to a runny consistency (see page 192). Put this in a new piping bag and use to flood the letter centres. Be careful not to let it overflow the sides.

5 Mix the remaining 50g of icing with red food colour and enough water to achieve a slight runny consistency. Put it in a fresh piping bag, snip off a small tip and pipe little dots into the still-wet pink icing of the letters. Let dry.

6 Arrange the cakes to spell out your personal message (or jumble them), in a gift box if you like.

Ribbon Rose Cup Cakes

These feature a very pretty type of rose made using a simple technique. As it looks like a piece of ribbon rolled together to form a little rosebud, I have called it a 'ribbon rose'.

FOR 12 CUP CAKES

about 200g sugar paste
red, pink and green food colours
icing sugar for dusting
12 cup cakes, made using ½
    recipe quantities Victoria
    sponge (see page 174),
    flavoured to choice, baked in
    silver metallic muffin cases,
    soaked with syrup and iced
    with pink and purple fondant
    icing (see page 188)
small amount of royal icing
    (see page 191)

EQUIPMENT

cling film
small non-stick plastic board
small rolling pin
leaf cutter
small kitchen knife
paper piping bag (see page 193)
pair of scissors

1 Mix about 75g of the sugar paste with red colour, 75g with pink and 50g with green. Always keep paste you are not using covered with cling film to prevent it drying out.

2 On a plastic board lightly dusted with icing sugar, roll a piece of pink or red sugar paste out to about 3cm (1¼ inches) wide, 8cm (3¼ inches) long and about 1mm (¹/₂₄ inch) thick. Trim the edges and fold the strip over in half lengthwise down its width, pinching it at intervals to get a pleated effect, as shown. Now roll the folded strip up from one side to the other and pinch off the excess at the bottom of the flower shape. Let dry. You'll need 6 pink and 6 red roses.

3 For the leaves, roll out a thin piece of green sugar paste and cut out 24 leaves using the leaf cutter. Mark the leaf veins down the middle using a small kitchen knife. Shape the leaves slightly with your fingers and let dry.

4 Once the roses and leaves are dry, stick them on top of the cup cakes using a dab of royal icing to fix them in place.

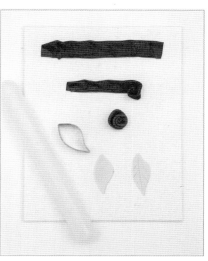

Rococo Cup Cakes

A lot of my designs are inspired by fashion and jewellery. The inspiration for these cup cakes comes from a photograph I saw in a bridal magazine of a beautiful French antique-style looped earring studded with little lilac blossoms and draped jewels, worn by a model in a frilled eau-de-Nil dress. The whole effect is very Marie Antoinette. I love the colour combination of green, lilac and gold. Let them eat cake...

FOR 12 CUP CAKES
about 150g sugar flower paste
purple and green food colours
icing sugar or cornflour, for dusting
small amount of royal icing
12 cup cakes (flavoured to your choice), made from
    ½ recipe quantities of Victoria sponge baked in
    gold cup cake cases, soaked with syrup and iced
    with eau-de-Nil coloured fondant icing, as
    described on pages 190–1
pink or silver sparkling sugar pearls

EQUIPMENT
small bowls
small plastic board
small rolling pin
cling film
petunia flower cutter
foam pad
bone tool
flower veiner
small painter's palette
small calyx cutter
paper piping bags (see page 193)
pair of scissors

1 Mix the flower paste with the purple food colour to produce a soft lilac shade.

2 On the plastic board lightly dusted with icing sugar or cornflour, roll some of this lilac paste out very thinly. Cover the rest with cling film to prevent it drying out.

3 Using the petunia cutter, cut out 12 large flower shapes, place them on top of the foam pad and smooth the edges using the bone tool. Press the flower veiner gently on top of each flower and place it into a well of a painter's palette to let it dry in a curved shape.

4 Roll out the remaining paste and, using a small calyx cutter, cut out about 120 small flowers. Slightly curve them between your fingers and let them dry. (You will need about 10 small flowers per cup cake.)

5 Mix a small amount of royal icing with purple food colour to a soft lilac shade and put into a piping bag. Snip a small tip off the bag and pipe the drapes and loops around the sides of each cup cake. First, divide the circumference of the cup cake into 10 even sections and mark them with small dots around edge. Pipe and lift your bag from dot to dot by letting the line fall down slightly. Let the first row of swags dry.

6 Once these are completely dry, pipe the next row of swags either in between or slightly lower than the previous one. In this way you will be able to create different patterns and designs.

7 Using small dabs of icing, stick one large flower in the middle of each cup cake and the little flowers evenly around the sides of each. Then arrange the sugar pearls in the centre of each flower.

8 Mix a small amount of icing with green food colour and put it into a fresh piping bag.

9 Snip the tip off in a V shape and pipe small leaves around all the flowers. (Be careful when lifting the cakes, as the piping around the sides will be very fragile.)

Spring Blossom Cup Cakes

Delicately handcrafted pastel-coloured spring flowers give these delicious chocolate cup cakes a fresh and romantic look. They look particularly pretty arranged on a vintage-style cake stand and are ideal for a spring tea or even a spring wedding in a beautiful country garden.

FOR 12 CUP CAKES
about 150g white sugar flower paste
small amount of white vegetable fat
violet, dusky-pink, green and yellow food colours
icing sugar or cornflour for dusting
small amount of royal icing (see page 191)
yellow blossom tint dusting colour
12 cup cakes made using ½ recipe quantities of rich dark chocolate sponge (see page 175), baked in silver muffin cases and iced with about 250g chocolate ganache (see page 180)

EQUIPMENT
cling film
non-stick board with holes (Celboard)
small rolling pin
small petunia cutter
flower foam pad with holes (Celpad)
bone tool (PME or JEM)
veining tool (JEM)
petal fluting/pointed end tool (JEM)
small bowls
palette knife
paper piping bags (see page 193)
small star piping tube
small primrose cutter
cocktail stick or Celstick
violet cutter
serrated and taper cone tool (PME)
stayfresh multi mat

1 Knead the sugar flower paste with a small amount of white vegetable fat until smooth and pliable. Divide it into 3 equal parts and mix one with violet and one with dusky pink to a light pastel shade. Keep the 3 pieces of paste separate, covered in cling film until later use.

FOR THE PETUNIAS
2 On the part of the plastic board with the largest hole, dusted with icing sugar, roll a small amount of the dusky-pink paste out until very thin. Turn the paste upside down and place the petunia cutter over the top with the knob of paste in the middle. Cut out the flower shape and transfer it on to the foam pad, placing the knob of paste inside the large hole.

3 Gently run the bone tool over the edges and then roll the veining tool across each petal. Gently shape

the centre of the flower around the bone tool and slightly curve the petals with your fingers. Repeat for about 12 petunias and let dry, keeping the rest of the paste covered with cling film.

4 Once they are dry, mix a small amount of royal icing with green food colour and put it in a piping bag fitted with a star piping tube. Pipe a small star inside the well of each flower.

5 Mix a small amount of royal icing with yellow food colour. Put it in a piping bag, cut off a small tip and pipe little yellow dots for the stamens on top of the green centres. Let dry.

FOR THE PRIMROSES

6 On the part of the plastic board with the medium-size hole, lightly dusted with icing sugar, roll out a small amount of the white sugar flower paste thinly. Turn the paste upside down and place the primrose cutter over the top with the knob of paste in the middle. Cut out the flower shape and transfer it to the foam pad, placing the knob of paste inside the medium-size hole.

7 Using a cocktail stick or Celstick, roll over each petal to stretch it. Pick up the flower with your fingers and gently push the serrated tip of the taper cone tool into the centre of the primrose. Repeat for about 24 primroses and let dry.

8 Once they are dry, dust the centres of the flowers lightly with the yellow blossom tint, using a fine brush.

9 Mix a small amount of icing with green food colour, put it in a piping bag and pipe a small dot into the centre of each primrose.

FOR THE VIOLETS

10 On the part of the plastic board with the smallest hole, lightly dusted with icing sugar, roll out a small amount of the violet sugar flower paste thinly. Turn the paste upside down and place the violet cutter over the top with the knob of paste in the middle.

11 Cut out the flower shape and transfer it on to the foam pad with the knob of paste facing up. Gently run the bone tool from the outer edge of each petal towards the middle. This will curve up the petals.

12 Pick up the violet blossom with your fingers and gently push the smooth end of the taper cone tool into the flower centre. Repeat for about 36 violets. Let dry.

TO FINISH

13 Mix a small amount of royal icing with yellow food colour and pipe a small dot into the middle of each flower, covering the hole.

14 Once all the flowers are dry, arrange them on top of the cup cakes.

Miniature Cakes

Pansy Pots

My parents, both dedicated hobby gardeners, were undoubtedly the inspiration for these adorable little cakes, as pansies are high on their list of favourite flowers. Whenever I go back home in spring, our garden is just full of their brilliant colours. It's no surprise, then, that I felt compelled to turn their passion into sweet treats as gifts for them. Make these cakes at least a day before you need them. The pansy flowers can be made well in advance, as they last for weeks.

FOR 12 CAKES

butter and flour for lining the moulds
1 recipe quantity rich dark chocolate cake mixture (see page 175)
100ml plain sugar syrup (see page 178)
500g white sugar paste
food colours (brown, orange, pink, yellow, violet, moss green)
1 teaspoon tylo powder (see step 6)
300g white flower paste
small amount of white vegetable fat
50g sieved apricot jam
250g chocolate-flavoured sugar paste
100g royal icing (see page 191)

EQUIPMENT

12 timbale moulds
wire cooling rack
pastry brush
cling film
small plastic board
pansy petal and leaf cutters
foam pad
bone tool
fine artist's brush
small painter's palette
black edible ink pen
small rolling pin
small kitchen knife
leaf veining mat
paper piping bag (page 193)

1 To bake the sponges: preheat the oven to 180°C, gas4. Grease 12 timbale moulds with butter and then dust them with flour, shaking out excess.

2 Make the sponge mixture as described on page 175 and then spoon just enough into the prepared timbale moulds to half fill them.

3 Bake in the preheated oven for about 15 minutes. Allow the cakes to cool a little on a wire rack and then turn them out of their moulds (see 1 overleaf).

4 Make the flowerpots: once the sponge cakes are cool, soak their tops with the sugar syrup using a pastry brush, wrap them in cling film and chill for at least 2 hours to firm them up.

5 Mix the white sugar paste with some brown and orange food colour until you achieve a nice terracotta colour.

6 Mix in the tylo powder (this is a hardening agent and will also help to make the paste more flexible and stable), wrap in cling film and allow the paste to rest for at least half an hour.

7 While the paste is resting, make the pansy flowers. Divide the white flower paste into 7 pieces. Keep 1 white and colour the remaining pieces with yellow, moss green and 2 different shades of pink and violet. Wrap the ones you aren't going to use immediately in cling film to prevent them from drying out.

8 Rub a thin layer of white vegetable fat over a plastic board to prevent the flower paste from sticking to it.

9 Roll out one colour of paste very thinly and, using a pansy petal cutter, cut out the petals. For one blossom you will need 2 large and 2 small teardrop-shaped petals and 1 large base petal as shown.

10 Place the petals on the foam pad and smooth the edges by using the bone tool (see 4).

11 Arrange the petals into a flower by placing the 2 small petals next to each other, slightly overlapping, and stick them together by brushing the sides where they touch with a little water. Place the 2 large petals to the left and to the right below the small petals, also overlapping and touching the sides. Use a little water to stick them to the small petals. Finally stick on the large base petal with a little bit of water (see 5) and push a little well into the centre, using the end of a brush or a pointed flower tool (see 6).

12 Place the flower into the well of a small painter's palette to let it dry (see 6). Repeat the procedure for all the flowers; you will need 6 flowers per pot.

13 Depending on the thickness of your paste, let them dry for at least 2–4 hours.

14 Once they are dry, paint some fine black lines into the centre using a black edible ink pen.

15 When the sponges are chilled, bring the jam to the boil in a small pan, turn the sponges upside down and brush sides and tops with jam.

16 Roll out the terracotta paste to about 3mm/ ⅛ inch thick and lay it over the upside-down sponges. Using a kitchen knife, trim off the excess paste and let the iced cakes set for at least 4 hours, until the paste feels firm to the touch.

17 Turn the cakes back over. Roll out some more of the terracotta paste to the same thickness as before and cut out 12 strips each 1cm/ ½ inch wide and about 15cm/ 6 inches long (they dry out very quickly, so it is best to work on 3 or 4 at a time).

18 Brush the top edge of each pot with a little water and stick the terracotta strip around it (see 2). If the strip is too long, trim off the excess with a small knife.

19 Roll a piece of chocolate-flavoured sugar paste into a ball and flatten it to a slight dome shape large enough to cover the sponge still showing inside the pot (see 3).

20 Brush with hot jam and stick the paste on top.

21 Before sticking the flowers on top of the pot, make the pansy leaves. Mix some of the flower paste with moss-green food colour and roll it out very thinly.

22 Cut out the leaves using a metal leaf cutter and place them on the foam pad.

23 Use the bone tool to smooth the edges and the veining mat to give them veins (see 8).

24 Stick the flowers and leaves on top of the flowerpots with little dabs of royal icing. While they are still soft, shape the leaves and make sure you have hardly any gaps between the flowers and the leaves (see 9).

MAKING THE PANSY POTS

'our garden is just full of their brilliant colours'

Mini Tea Rose Wedding Cakes

Miniature wedding cakes provide a modern twist to the traditional large cake and are ideal for smaller wedding receptions. Instead of having one large cake to cut, the bride and groom can serve individual cakes to each of their guests. This particular cake is inspired by the lovely ceramic artistry of the tea set on which it is served. Make the cake at least a day in advance. The flowers can be made well before you need them, as they will last for weeks.

FOR 6 CAKES

1 sheet of sponge cake, 30 x 40cm/ 12 x 16 inches, using 2 recipe quantities of basic Victoria sponge mixture, flavoured and soaked to your choice (see page 174)

100g sieved apricot jam

icing sugar for dusting

500g white sugar paste

50g sugar paste

violet food colour

50g royal icing (see page 191)

edible gold lustre powder

1 teaspoon clear alcohol (such as vodka)

30 mini roses made from sugar paste coloured dusky pink (see pages 197–9)

36 rose leaves made from moss-green sugar paste (see pages 197–9)

EQUIPMENT

cling film

round pastry cutters, 7.5cm/3 inch and 3.5cm/1½ inch diameter

small saucepan

pastry brush

small rolling pin

5mm/¼ inch guide sticks

2 cake smoothers

small kitchen knife

greaseproof paper

small plastic board

miniature blossom cutter

bone tool

paper piping bags (see page 193)

fine artist's brush

1 Wrap the soaked sheet of sponge in cling film and chill for about 2 hours until firm.

2 Using 7.5cm/3 inch and 3.5cm/1½ inch round pastry cutters, cut out 6 rounds in each size from the firmed-up sponge.

3 Bring the jam to the boil in a small pan and, using a pastry brush, brush each round all over with the hot jam.

4 On a work surface dusted with icing sugar, roll out the white sugar paste to 5mm/¼ inch thick using guide sticks and cover each of the rounds with the paste, as described on page 187.

5 Use the cake smoothers to straighten the sides and tops of each of the cakes.

6 Trim off excess paste using a small kitchen knife, place the cakes on a sheet of greaseproof paper and let set for a day.

7 Make the little lilac blossoms by mixing the sugar paste with a little bit of violet food colour. Roll it out thinly on a plastic board dusted with icing sugar. Cut out

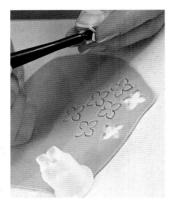

the blossoms using a mini blossom cutter and shape them with a bone tool as shown. Let dry overnight.

8 Pipe a small dot of royal icing in the centre of each of the large cakes and then place a small cake on top.

9 Pipe a border (see page 194) around the base of each tier and let it dry.

10 Mix some gold lustre powder to a paste with a little clear alcohol and paint the piped border using a fine artist's brush.

11 Stick the lilac blossoms, mini roses and leaves on top of the cake with little dabs of royal icing.

Miniature Wedding Cakes

As a specialist in making wedding cakes, I have noticed right from my very first commissions that although brides these days are still looking for something traditional, more and more they want a cake with an unusual twist to it. As this idea provides both a cutting cake and individual cakes that can be used as favours at the same time, it is no surprise that it has become one of my bestsellers. Another advantage of this cake is that you can offer your guests a choice of different cake flavours.

It is best to make as much of this as possible in advance: try to start making the top tier and the miniature cakes 2 days ahead, the sugar flowers at least 1 day ahead and the chocolate ganache half a day.

**FOR ABOUT 80 MINIATURE CAKES
AND ONE 15CM/6 INCH TOP TIER**

1 sheet of orange-flavoured sponge cake, 30 x 40 cm/ 12 x 16 inches, using 2 recipe quantities of basic Victoria sponge mixture (see page 174)

1 sheet of lemon-flavoured sponge cake, 30 x 40 cm/ 12 x 16 inches, using 2 recipe quantities of basic Victoria sponge mixture (see page 174)

15cm/6 inch round chocolate sponge cake, using 1 recipe quantity basic Victoria sponge mixture (see page 174)

150ml sugar syrup (see page 178) flavoured with finely grated orange zest and juice and Grand Marnier

100g orange marmalade

150g orange-flavoured buttercream (see page 179)

150ml sugar syrup (see page 178) flavoured with finely grated lemon zest, lemon juice and Limoncello

150g lemon curd (I use best-quality bought)

150g lemon-flavoured buttercream (see page 179)

100ml plain sugar syrup (see page 178)

250g chocolate ganache (see page 180), flavoured with peppermint liqueur

450g white marzipan

5kg white sugar paste

150g sieved apricot jam

250g royal icing (see page 191)

icing sugar for dusting

80 5-petal flowers (see pages 195) in two different shades of pink

green food colour

EQUIPMENT

large serrated knife

pastry brush

cling film

15cm/6 inch round cake board

round pastry cutter, 5cm/2 inch diameter

2 large trays

large rolling pin

5mm/¼ inch guide sticks

15m satin ribbon, 15mm thick, in two shades of pink

small saucepan

kitchen knife

cake smoothers

greaseproof paper

paper piping bag (see page 193)

4-tier Perspex cake stand (try to hire one from a local cake-maker)

25 bright pink fresh roses and 25 pale pink fresh roses, plus some more petals, to decorate

TO FILL THE CAKES:

1 Once your sponge cakes are cool, trim the top crust off each of them using a large serrated knife.

2 For the orange cakes, slice the sheet of orange sponge in half and soak the tops of both layers with the orange-flavoured sugar syrup.

3 Spread one layer with orange marmalade then with orange buttercream, and sandwich the other on top. Wrap in cling film and chill for at least an hour until firm.

4 For the lemon cakes, slice the sheet of lemon sponge in half and soak the tops of both layers with the lemon-flavoured sugar syrup.

5 Spread one layer with lemon curd, then with lemon buttercream and sandwich the other on top. Wrap in cling film and chill for at least an hour until firm.

6 For the 15cm/6 inch top tier, slice the round chocolate sponge into 3 layers and soak each one with the plain sugar syrup.

7 Layer the sponges with the peppermint-flavoured chocolate ganache. Chill for at least 1 hour until the ganache has set.

8 Once set, stick the chocolate cake on to a 15cm/6 inch round cake board with a dab of the ganache and coat it with ganache once more until even and smooth. Chill again.

9 Take the chilled orange and lemon sponge out of the fridge and cut out rounds from them using a 5cm/2 inch diameter pastry cutter. Each sheet should produce about 40. Place them on a tray, wrap in cling film and chill again until needed.

TO DECORATE THE CAKES:

10 For the top tier: remove the chocolate cake from the fridge and cover it in thin coat of chocolate ganache to help the marzipan stick.

11 Cover the cake with the marzipan and then 500g of the white sugar paste as described on pages 184-5. Let everything set for 1 day

12 Once set, lay some dark-pink satin ribbon around the sides and fix in place with a dot of royal icing.

13 For the miniature cakes: bring the apricot jam to the boil in a small pan. Remove the little cakes

from the fridge and brush the tops and the sides with the jam, using a pastry brush.

14 On a surface dusted with icing sugar, roll out some of the white sugar paste, using 5mm/¼ inch guide sticks.

15 Cover each cake with the sugar paste and trim off excess. Use cake smoothers to smooth the top and the sides. Place the cakes on a tray lined with greaseproof paper and let set overnight.

16 Once set, attach a small piece of satin ribbon around the base of each tier with a dab of royal icing. Use one shade for each flavour, so you will be able to differentiate the cake types when serving them.

17 Stick a 5-petal flower in a shade matching that of the ribbon on top of each cake with a dab of icing.

18 Mix a little bit of royal icing with some green food colour, snip the tip of a paper icing bag in a 'V' shape and pipe small leaves around each flower.

ARRANGING THE CAKES:

19 Place the 15cm/6 inch cake on the top tier of a cake stand. Arrange the little cakes on the tiers below, leaving some gaps for fresh roses.

20 Arrange some fresh roses and petals all over the cake stand and the top tier.

Stripy Rose Cakes

Smart stripes and candy pink are more fashionable than ever, and help turn these pretty pastries into couture cakes. I recently made these cakes for a friend and, for a change, decorated them with stripes in vivid rainbow colours – they were a great hit.

FOR ABOUT 15

½ sheet of sponge cake,
   30 x 40cm/12 x 16 inches,
   using 2 recipe quantities of
   basic Victoria sponge mixture,
   flavoured, soaked and
   filled to your choice
   (see page 174)
150g sieved apricot jam
icing sugar for dusting
750g white sugar paste
250g royal icing (see page 191)
pink food colour
15 pink sugar paste roses with
   green calyxes (see page 199)

EQUIPMENT

cling film
5cm/2 inch round pastry cutter
small saucepan
pastry brush
small rolling pin
5mm/¼ inch guide sticks
small kitchen knife
2 cake smoothers
greaseproof paper
small palette knife
paper piping bags (see page 193)

Make these at least a day
in advance.

1 Wrap the soaked and filled sheet of sponge in cling film and chill for about 2 hours until firm.

2 Using a 5cm/2 inch round pastry cutter, cut out about 15 circles.

3 Bring the apricot jam to the boil in a small pan and, using a pastry brush, brush each cake all over with the jam.

4 On a surface dusted with icing sugar, roll out the sugar paste to 5mm/¼ inch thick using guide sticks. Cover each cake with the paste as described on page 182–3.

5 Trim off the excess paste using a small kitchen knife.

6 Use the cake smoothers to straighten the sides and top of the cakes. Place on a sheet of greaseproof paper and let dry for 1 day.

7 Once the icing has set firm, fill one piping bag with soft-peak icing in pastel pink and another with soft-peak icing in bright pink.

8 Pipe lines as shown, starting at the top in the centre, lifting the bag and bringing it slowly down to the bottom of the cake. Touch the end point and stop piping (see Basic Piping Techniques on page 194). Pipe one line next to the other in alternating colours, keeping the lines nice and straight.

9 Finish the lines by piping small dots in the same colours along the base.

10 Place a sugar paste rose on top of each cake and stick it on with a dab of royal icing.

Chocolate Bow Candy Cakes

These cakes make great gifts for any occasion and are also ideal for a small wedding, as you can make a tiered miniature wedding cake per guest instead of one large wedding cake. As they travel well and look very pretty in a clear gift box, they also make stunning wedding favours.

FOR ABOUT 6 MINI TIERED CAKES
about 250g ready-made
   dark-brown chocolate-
   flavoured sugar paste
gum tragacanth
icing sugar for dusting
edible glue
six 7.5cm/3-inch and six
   3.5cm/1½-inch round cakes,
   made from a 30cm/12-inch
   square rich dark chocolate
   cake (see page 175), flavoured
   and soaked to choice, then
   covered with marzipan and
   pastel-blue, green and yellow
   sugar paste (2 of each type
   of cake in each colour,
   see pages 181–3)

small amount of royal icing
   (see page 191)
dark-brown and willow-green
   (Wilton) food colours

EQUIPMENT
cling film or damp cloth
small non-stick plastic board
small rolling pin
small kitchen knife
design wheeler (PME)
small brush
kitchen paper
bow cutter (JEM)

FOR THE BLUE CAKES
1 Mix the dark brown chocolate sugar paste with a little gum tragacanth. Wrap in cling film and let rest for about half an hour until the paste is flexible.

2 On a plastic board dusted with icing sugar, roll out the paste and cut it into strips 15mm/⅜ inch wide, then roll the design wheeler along the edges.

3 To make each bow, cut a strip 10cm (4 inches) long and turn upside down. Fold both ends over and glue down in the middle, supporting the loops with kitchen paper. Cut another strip about 3cm/1¼ inches long, fold it over the joint and fix with edible glue. Let dry.

4 Cut 4 strips about 15cm/6 inches in length and lay them down the sides of the cake, fixing them with edible glue. Cut 4 thin strips to place in between the spaces at the bottom.

5 To finish each bow, cut 2 more pieces of brown paste about 4cm/1½ inches long and snip the ends in a V shape. Stick on the top tier with edible glue, then add the bow.

FOR THE GREEN CAKES

6 On a plastic board dusted with icing sugar, thinly roll out the brown paste. Cut out the shapes for the bows using the bow cutter. Assemble the bows as before. Let dry.

7 Divide the top tier of the green cake into 3 and the bottom tier into 5 even parts and mark them with small dots around the edge.

8 Roll out another piece of brown paste and cut out strips about 1cm/½ inch wide and 4–6cm/1½–2½ inches in length.

9 Twist each strip with your fingers and attach to the sides of the cake with edible glue.

10 Now stick the brown bows on top of the joins, using a small amount of chocolate-brown royal icing.

11 Mix a small amount of icing with green colour to soft-peak consistency (see page 192) and pipe small dots around the base of each tier.

FOR THE YELLOW CAKES

12 On a plastic board dusted with icing sugar, thinly roll out the brown paste. Cut out a 5mm/1/4 inch thin strip to go around the base of the bottom tier and a 2.5cm/1 inch thick strip to go around the base of the top tier. Fix them both in place with edible glue.

13 To make the bow, cut out a 1.5cm/5⁄8-inch wide and 10cm/4-inch long strip from the paste, fold both ends over to the middle and glue them down, supporting the loops with kitchen paper. Cut another strip about 3cm/1¼ inches in length, fold it over the join and fix it with some edible glue. Let dry.

14 To finish the bow, cut 2 more pieces of brown paste of about 4cm/1½ inches in length and snip the ends off in a V shape. Place them on the side of top tier with brown icing or edible glue and stick the bow on top.

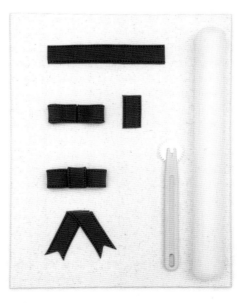

Chocolate Hearts

These little French-style chocolate heart cakes make a delightful alternative to chocolate or chocolate truffles. I used an old-fashioned crimping technique for the border design on the monogram heart, which gives this classic design a touch of 'retro revival'.

FOR 24 SMALL CAKES

24 small cakes made using 1½ recipe quantities of rich dark chocolate sponge (see page 175), baked in miniature heart-shaped baking tins (about 5cm/2 inches across)

2 tablespoon sieved apricot jam

icing sugar for dusting

about 1kg dark-brown chocolate-flavoured sugar paste

a little edible glue or alcohol

small amount of royal icing (see page 191)

pink food colour

about 200g white sugar paste

pink edible lustre

EQUIPMENT

small kitchen knife

small saucepan

pastry brush

rolling pin

5mm/¼-inch marzipan spacers

serrated crimping tool

small rolling pin with a lined surface

paper piping bags (see page 193)

pair of scissors

small heart cutter

fine artist's brush

1 Level the top of the heart sponges by trimming off the top crust with a kitchen knife. Gently heat up the apricot jam and thinly brush it all over the little sponges.

2 On a smooth surface dusted with icing sugar, roll out the chocolate sugar paste between the marzipan spacers to a piece large enough to cover the top and sides of the cakes. Lay it over them and carefully push it down the sides. Trim the excess paste off using a kitchen knife.

FOR THE MONOGRAM HEART CAKES

3 Roll a small amount of chocolate paste to a sausage long enough to cover the circumference of the heart. Brush the base of each cake thinly with edible glue or alcohol and lay the sausage around the sides.

4 Gently push the crimper all around the base, creating a continuous patterned border.

5 Mix a small amount of royal icing with pink food colour and a little water to produce soft-peak consistency (see page 192) and put it into a piping bag. Pipe the monogram on top of each cake.

FOR THE DOTTED HEART CAKES

6 Mix the white sugar paste with a small amount of pink food colour and roll it out on the plastic board dusted with icing sugar to a strip long enough to cover the base of each heart. Roll once over that with the lined rolling pin to give it a lined pattern, then cut it into a long strip about 1cm/½ inch) wide.

7 Brush a thin strip around the base of each cake with edible glue and lay the pink strip around it.

8 Pipe little dots of pink royal icing all over the top of the cakes. Let dry.

FOR THE HEARTS ON HEART CAKES

9 On a plastic board dusted lightly with icing sugar, roll out some pink sugar paste until very thin. Using the heart cutter, cut out little heart shapes and dust them with pink lustre.

10 Brush the back of each heart thinly with edible glue and randomly arrange the pink hearts all over the cakes. Let dry.

White Spring Posies

This is a unique idea for miniature wedding cakes or bridesmaids' gifts. You can use flowers to match your bridal bouquet and recreate an edible version. As these are incredibly time-consuming to make, I recommend using them for smaller weddings or events.

FOR 16 CAKES
about 1 packet (250g) of white sugar flower paste (Squire's Kitchen)
small amount of white vegetable fat
icing sugar or cornflour, for dusting
about 1kg white sugar paste
green food colour
16 miniature cakes (5cm/2-inch diameter), made from a 25cm/10 inch square of basic Victoria sponge mixture, flavoured and soaked to your choice, covered with marzipan and a thin layer of white sugar paste (see pages 174–183)
edible glue
small amount of royal icing (see page 191)

EQUIPMENT
small plastic board
small rolling pin
small stephanotis cutter
cling film
stay-fresh mat
foam pad
flower/leaf shaper tool (PME)
cake smoother
small kitchen knife
small artist's brush
paper piping bag (see page 193)
pair of scissors

TO MAKE THE FLOWERS (YOU WILL NEED ABOUT 30 PER CAKE)
1 Knead the flower paste with a little white vegetable fat until smooth and pliable.

2 On a plastic board lightly dusted with icing sugar or cornflour, roll a small piece of flower paste out very thinly. Cut out the little flowers using the stephanotis cutter (see 1, page 97). Keep the remaining paste covered in cling film to prevent it drying out.

3 Keeping the flowers not being used covered with the stay-fresh mat, place a few at a time on the foam pad and push a line from the middle down each petal using the shaper tool (see 2, page 97). This way the petals will slightly curve inwards. Let dry.

4 Pipe little dots of royal icing into the centres of each flower (see 3, page 97). Let dry.

TO MAKE THE FLOWER STEMS

5 Divide the sugar paste into 4 even pieces and mix three of them with various amounts of green food colour to give 3 different shades of green. Leave the rest white.

6 To make the stems, roll a small piece of each colour green out to a thin sausage using the cake smoother, and cut into pieces long enough to cover the sides of the cakes (see 4).

7 Brush the sides of each cake with edible glue and stick the stems around in alternating shades of green (see 5). Push them flat on to the side of the cake using a cake smoother (see 6). Trim off excess at the top with a sharp knife (see 7).

TO FINISH THE TOP OF THE CAKES WITH FLOWERS

8 Roll a small piece of white sugar paste to a ball, and push it down to a dome shape. It should be large enough to cover the top of a cake. Stick it on top using a dab of royal icing (see 8). Do the same for the other cakes.

9 Using little dabs of royal icing, stick one layer of flowers all over each dome (see 9). Stick a second layer of flowers in between the gaps of the first. Let dry.

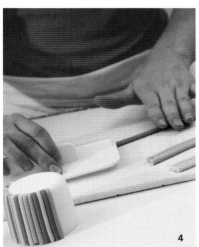

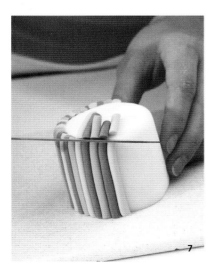

Large Cakes

Valentine's Heart

It is easy to make a simple heart-shaped cake look very special indeed. The romantic floral border cascading down the sides of the cake makes a striking frame for a personal message or someone's name on top, so it could be used as a billet-doux for any sort of romantic occasion. Make this cake at least one day in advance.

FOR AN 8 INCH (20CM) CAKE (ABOUT 25 PARTY PORTIONS)

750g pastel-pink sugar paste
300g royal icing (see page 191)
two 20cm/8 inch round sponge cakes, using 2 recipe quantities of basic Victoria sponge mixture, flavoured to your choice (see page 174)
150ml sugar syrup (see page 178), flavoured to your choice
250g chosen filling (buttercream, see page 179, or chocolate ganache, see page 180)
icing sugar for dusting
600g white marzipan
2 tablespoons clear alcohol (such as vodka)
selection of food colours

EQUIPMENT

30cm/12 inch round or heart-shaped thick cake board
pink satin ribbon, 15mm thick
flower nail
greaseproof paper
metal piping nozzles for flower-making (see page 195)
paper piping bags (see page 193)
large serrated knife
large palette knife
20cm/8 inch heart-shaped cake board
pastry brush
rolling pin
5mm/¼ inch guide sticks
kitchen knife
2 cake smoothers
tilting turntable

1 Cover the 30cm/12 inch thick cake board with 150g of the pink sugar paste and the ribbon, following the instructions on page 186. Let set overnight.

2 Using the flower nail lined with pieces of greaseproof paper, royal icing and a selection of different piping nozzles, make a selection of sugar flowers, enough to cover the sides of your cake, as described on page 195. Leave to dry overnight.

3 Trim the top crust off both sponges using a serrated knife. Cut 2 heart shapes out of the sponge using the 20cm/8 inch heart-shaped cake board as a template.

4 Soak and layer the 2 heart-shaped sponges with your chosen filling.

5 Coat the outside of the cake with the same filling and chill for at least 2 hours.

6 Once chilled, give the cake another coat of ganache or buttercream to make the marzipan stick to the cake.

7 On a surface dusted with icing sugar, roll the marzipan out between 5mm/¼ inch guide sticks using a large rolling pin.

8 Using the rolling pin to help you, lay the marzipan over the top of the cake and push it down the side. Trim away the excess with a knife.

9 Use the cake smoothers to make the top and sides nice and even. Let set overnight.

10 Brush the outside of the marzipanned cake with a little alcohol to make the sugar paste stick to the marzipan.

11 Cover the cake with the rest of the sugar paste following the same technique as for the marzipan. Let everything harden overnight.

12 Once hardened, pipe a dot of icing in the centre of the prepared thick cake board and place the cake on top. Let it set for 1 hour to make sure the cake sticks firmly to the board.

13 Prepare 3 piping bags filled with soft-peak royal icing in 3 different shades of pink.

14 Place the cake, on its board, on top of a tilting turntable. Tilt it slightly to the side away from you and then start piping lines down the sides, starting from the top edge down to the bottom edge and alternating the three shades. (See 1 and Basic Piping Techniques on page 194.)

15 Pipe a border of matching dots along the bottom of the cake (see 2).

16 Arrange the sugar flowers along the top edge to form a frame around the heart shape, using royal icing to stick the flowers in place (see 3).

17 Fill another piping bag with green stiff-peak royal icing and pipe a couple of green leaves between the flowers, as described on page 11.

Three-column Wedding Cake

This is a rather unconventional wedding cake, as the tiers are placed next to each other instead of being stacked. Decorating cakes with fresh flowers has become very popular and the beautiful cascading roses here were kindly arranged by one of London's top floral designers, Rob Van Helden, whose glamorous creations are second to none. Your florist should be able to supply the oasis dome shape holders, or ask them to arrange the flowers for you. Make sure the roses haven't been treated with chemicals as they come in contact with the cake. Make this cake at least three days in advance.

FOR ABOUT 100 PORTIONS
3.5kg white sugar paste
food colours (pink, orange, yellow)
6 sheets of sponge cake, 30 x 40cm/12 x 16 inches, each using 2 recipe quantities of basic Victoria sponge mixture, flavoured to your choice (see page 174)
500ml sugar syrup (see page 178), flavoured to your choice
1.5kg buttercream (see page 179) or other filling of your choice
icing sugar for dusting
3kg white marzipan
500g royal icing (see page 191)
a little clear alcohol, such as vodka

EQUIPMENT
cling film
50cm/20 inch thick round cake board
about 2m pastel-pink satin ribbon, 15mm wide
large serrated knife
three 15cm/6 inch thick round cake boards
small kitchen knife
pastry brush
small and large palette knives
large rolling pin
5mm/1/4 inch guide sticks
2 cake smoothers
paper piping bags (page 193)
3 small oasis dome flower holders
three 10cm/4 inch thin round cake boards
about 100 fresh roses in pastel yellow, peach and pink

1 At least 2 days ahead, colour your sugar paste: mix about 2kg with pink food colour, 1kg with orange and 500g yellow. Wrap separately in cling film until use.

2 Use about 500g of the pink paste to cover a 50cm/20 inch cake board and then decorate the sides with pastel-pink satin ribbon as described on page 18. Let dry for at least 2 days.

3 Also at least 2 days ahead, trim the top crust of each sponge sheet using the serrated knife.

4 Using a 15cm/6 inch round cake board as a template, lay it on top of each sponge sheet and cut three 15cm/6 inch circles out of each sheet (18 in total.)

5 You will need 1 tier consisting of 3 sponge circles, 1 tier consisting of 6 sponge circles and 1 tier consisting of 9 sponge circles.

6 Using a pastry brush, soak the top of each tier with sugar syrup and, using a palette knife, fill each tier with the filling of your choice as described on page 184. Place each tier on a 15cm/6 inch round cake board, fixing it in place with a dab of buttercream or chosen filling.

7 Cover all the cakes with marzipan as described on page 185 and let set for at least a day.

8 Next day, cover the cakes with sugar paste as described on page 185. Use the yellow paste for the small tier, the orange paste for the middle tier and the pink paste for the large tier. Let set for at least a day.

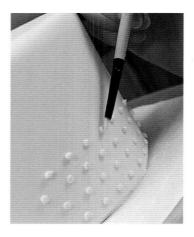

9 Once set, fill 3 paper piping bags with soft-peak royal icing of the same colour as the different sugar pastes and pipe small dots evenly all over the cakes. Should any of your dots form a peak, push it down with a damp brush while the icing is still wet, as shown above. Finish the top edge with a piped border of royal icing as described on page 194. Let dry for a couple of hours.

10 Pipe some royal icing on top of the large iced cake board to make the cakes stick to the board and position the three iced cakes as centrally as possible on top, using the large palette knife.

11 Soak the oasis dome flower holders in water and place them on top of the cake with a thin 4 inch (10cm) round cake board underneath to prevent the water from running on to the cake.

12 The flowers should stay fresh for up to 1 day, so if your wedding starts in the afternoo I would recommend you arrange the flowers no earlier than the late morning of the event. Cut the stems of each rose down to about 5cm/2 inches from the head.

13 Stick the roses into the dome-shaped holders and lay some roses loosely on top of the cakes so that they are cascading from the top tier over the middle tier down to the bottom tier. Scatter some rose petals randomly over the cake board.

14 Remember to ensure that the flowers are removed from the cakes before they are cut and eaten.

Gift Box Cake

If you are invited to a birthday party and you don't really know what to bring along, this cake is the ideal solution. Not only does it look like a genuine gift box, but the shimmering satin-like bow combined with the playful pink polka-dot design turns this simple cake into a funkily appealing present for people of all types and all ages. Make the bow at least 3 days ahead and the cake at least 2 days.

FOR A 20CM/8 INCH SQUARE CAKE (ABOUT 36 PORTIONS)

1.5kg white sugar paste
food colours (mint-green and pink)
1 tablespoon Tylo Powder
aqua shimmer powder
2 tablespoons clear alcohol, such as vodka
two 20cm/8 inch square sponge cakes, using 2 recipe quantities of basic Victoria sponge mixture, flavoured to your choice (see page 174)
150ml sugar syrup (see page 178), flavoured to your choice
250g filling of your choice (butter cream, see page 179 or chocolate ganache, (see page 180)
icing sugar for dusting
750g white marzipan
small amount of stiff-peak royal icing (see page 191)

EQUIPMENT

cling film
small rolling pin
small plastic board
small kitchen knife
thick soft artist's brush
tissue paper
greaseproof paper
20cm/8 inch square cake board
serrated knife
pastry brush
large palette knife
5mm/¼ inch guide sticks
large rolling pin
2 cake smoothers
selection of small round cutters in various sizes
paper piping bag (see page 193)

Start by making the loop for the sugar bow at least 3 days ahead

1 Mix about 500g of the white sugar paste with a little bit of mint-green food colour until the paste is a light green in colour. Knead the Tylo Powder into the paste (it is a hardening agent and will make the paste more flexible and stable), wrap it in cling film and let it rest for about half an hour.

2 Once rested, take a piece of the paste and you will feel how the paste has become a lot more flexible for moulding and shaping. Using a small rolling pin, roll a piece of paste out on a plastic board until very thin. Using a small sharp knife, cut a strip about 5 x 15cm/2 x 6 inches out of the paste.

3 Remove the trimmings and dust the strip with the aqua shimmer, using a thick soft artist's brush (see 1 opposite).

4 Turn the strip upside-down (see 2). Roll up some tissue paper into a cylinder about 5cm/2 inches in diameter, place it in the middle of the strip of paste and wrap the paste around it as shown (see 3). Pinch both ends together, using a little water or alcohol to make them stick. Transfer to a piece of greaseproof paper. Repeat this procedure again for the other half of the bow. Let both dry for at least 3 days.

PREPARE THE SPONGE CAKES:
5 Trim the top crust of both sponges, using the serrated knife. Soak them with sugar syrup and layer both with your chosen filling, as described on page 184.

6 Coat the outside of the cake with the same filling and chill for at least 2 hours.

7 Once chilled, take the cake out of the fridge, place it on top of an 20cm/8 inch cake board and give it another coat of ganache or buttercream to make the marzipan stick to the cake.

8 On a surface dusted with icing sugar, roll out the marzipan between 5mm/¼ inch guide sticks using a large rolling pin.

9 Lay the marzipan over the top of the cake and push down the side. Trim away excess marzipan with a knife. Use the cake smoothers to make the top and sides nice and even.

10 Brush the outside of the marzipanned cake with a little alcohol to make the sugar paste stick to the marzipan.

11 Cover the cake with 900g sugar paste following the same technique as for the marzipan. Let set overnight.

DECORATE THE CAKE:
12 Roll out the leftover green sugar paste for the bow and cut out 2 long strips of the same width as the bow and long enough to reach from one side of the cake to the other.

13 Dust each strip with the aqua shimmer as before (see 1). Using alcohol to stick the paste to the

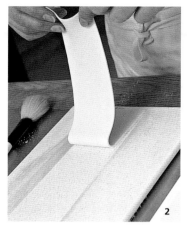

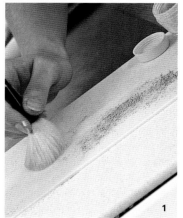

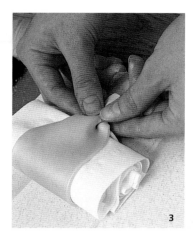

cake, lay the green sugar paste strips across and over the cake and pinch both strips together where they meet at the top of the cake (see 4 and 5). Trim the excess paste at the sides using a small knife.

14 Colour half of the remaining white sugar paste pale pink and the other half bright pink.

15 Roll the paste out on a small plastic board and cut out circles in different sizes using round cutters.

16 Arrange these randomly on the white parts of the cake (see 6), using some clear alcohol or water to make them stick.

17 Place the bow on top of the cake and fix it with a dab of royal icing.

18 For the end pieces of the bow, roll out another piece of paste as before and cut out 2 strips about 5 x 12cm/2 x 5 inches. Cut a 'V' into one end of each and pinch the other ends together. Stick to the bow with royal icing and lay them on top of the cake in a wavy shape.

19 Finally, roll out another small piece of green paste, dust with shimmer and wrap it around the middle of the bow.

Pink Wedding Cake

This gorgeous and girly creation of pastel-pink icing and white hydrangea sugar blossoms will help give any wedding that 'fairytale come true' feeling. Make this cake at least 3 days in advance. For an even more magical effect, you can sprinkle the white blossom with some white edible glitter while it is still wet.

FOR ABOUT 130 PORTIONS

5kg pastel-pink sugar paste
two 15cm/6 inch round sponge
   cakes, each using 1 recipe
   quantity of basic Victoria
   sponge mixture, flavoured to
   your choice (see page 174)
two 20cm/8 inch round sponge
   cakes, each using 1⅓ recipe
   quantities of basic Victoria
   sponge mixture, flavoured to
   your choice (see page 174)
two 25cm/10 inch round sponge
   cakes, each using 1½ recipe
   quantity of basic Victoria
   sponge mixture, flavoured to
   your choice (see page 174)
two 30cm/12 inch round sponge
   cakes, each using 2 recipe
   quantities of basic Victoria
   sponge mixture, flavoured to
   your choice (see page 174)
700ml sugar syrup (see page 178),
   flavoured to your choice
2kg buttercream (see page 179) or
   other filling of your choice
5kg marzipan
icing sugar for dusting
1kg royal icing (see page 191) for
   making the flowers
pink food colour

EQUIPMENT

40cm/16 inch round cake board
large serrated knife
pastry brush
large palette knife
about 4m white satin ribbon,
   15mm wide
15cm/6 inch thin round
   cake board
20cm/8 inch thin round
   cake board
25cm/10 inch thin round
   cake board
30cm/12 inch thin round
   cake board
large rolling pin
5mm/¼ inch guide sticks
2 cake smoothers
paper piping bags (see page 193)
piping nozzles (Wilton 103,
   PME, etc.)
flower nail
greaseproof paper
turntable
12 plastic dowels

1 Cover a 40cm/16 inch cake board with 350g pink sugar paste (see page 186). Cover sides with white ribbon.

2 You'll need 4 cake tiers, each consisting of 3 layered sponges (see above). Trim, soak and fill each tier as on page 184, then set it on an appropriate thin cake board. Chill.

3 Cover each tier with marzipan as on page 185. Let set overnight.

4 Pipe the hydrangea blossoms in different sizes using stiff royal icing. Make as 5-petal flowers (see page 195), but pipe only 4 petals. Mix a little of the icing with pink food colour and pipe the stamens in the centres. Let dry overnight.

5 Next day, cover each cake with pink sugar paste as on page 185. Let it set for one more night.

6 Once set, assemble the tiers and the cake board on top of each other as described on page 187.

7 Arrange ribbon around base of each tier. Stick flowers along the sides of each with stiff royal icing.

English Rose Wedding Cake

I recently saw a wallpaper design by Cath Kidston in an interiors magazine which has inspired this cake. I simply love the old-fashioned effect, it's so beautifully British and makes me think of English rose gardens. The technique used for painting the flowers on the cake is called 'brush embroidery'. If you haven't done this before, you might find it a bit difficult at the beginning, so I suggest you try it out on a cake board iced with sugar paste first until you are happy with the results, before you start with the cake. Make this cake at least 3 days in advance.

FOR 110 PORTIONS

3.5kg white sugar paste
food colours (pink, yellow
   and green)
two 15cm/6 inch round sponge
   cakes, each using 1 recipe
   quantity of basic Victoria
   sponge mixture, flavoured to
   your choice (see page 174)
two 23cm/9 inch round sponge
   cakes, each using 1½ recipe
   quantities of basic Victoria
   sponge mixture, flavoured to
   your choice (see page 174)
two 30cm/12 inch round sponge
   cakes, using 2 recipe quantities
   of basic Victoria sponge
   mixture, flavoured to your
   choice (see page 174)
500ml sugar syrup (see page 178),
   flavoured to your choice
1.5 kg buttercream (see page 179)
   or other filling of your choice
icing sugar for dusting
3kg white marzipan
500g royal icing (see page 191)

EQUIPMENT

about 1.5m bright pink satin
   ribbon, 30mm wide

about 1.5m bright pink satin
   ribbon, 15mm wide
one 40cm/16 inch thick round
   cake board
1 thin 15cm/6 inch round
   cake board
1 thin 23cm/9 inch round
   cake board
1 thin 30cm/12 inch round
   cake board
large serrated knife
pastry brush
large palette knife
large rolling pin
5mm/¼ inch guide sticks
2 cake smoothers
rose and rose leaf embossers
paper piping bags (see page 193)
fine artist's brush
turntable
two thick 7cm/3 inch round
   cake boards
two thick 15cm/6 inch round
   cake boards
two thick 23cm/9 inch round
   cake boards
needles
8 plastic dowels
scissors

1 Mix about 350g of white sugar paste with pink food colour until it has a deep fuchsia-pink colour, similar to that of the ribbon you are using. Use this paste to cover a 40cm/16 inch thick round cake board as described on page 186. Cover the sides of the board with the 15mm wide satin ribbon.

2 You will need 3 cake tiers, each consisting of 3 layered sponges, one 15cm/6 inches round, one 23cm/9 inches round and one 30cm/12 inches round. Trim, soak and fill each tier as described on page 16, then set on an appropriate thin cake board.

3 Cover each cake with marzipan as described on page 185 and let it set overnight.

4 Before covering the cakes with sugar paste, have rose and rose leaf embossers ready. Cover one cake with white sugar paste at a time, as described on page 185.

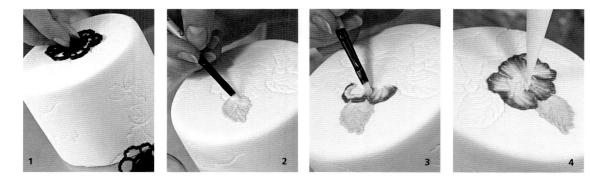

5 While the paste is still soft, push the embossers carefully into the paste of one cake to create an all-over rose and leaf design (see 1). Repeat for the other cakes and leave them to dry overnight.

6 Colour your royal icing and prepare your icing bags. You will need several piping bags filled with soft-peak royal icing in each of the following colours: fuchsia pink, pastel pink, green and yellow.

7 Start with the green leaves: pipe the outline of the leaf shape using the green icing. Take a fine artist's brush and dampen it with water. Use the brush to pull the icing from the outside into the middle of the leaf (see 2), which will create the veins of the leaves. Repeat for all the leaves, cleaning your brush from time to time.

8 When finished with the leaves, pipe the pink flowers: pipe each rose a petal at a time. Pipe one line of fuchsia-pink icing on the outline of a petal and pipe another line of pastel-pink icing next to it on the inside of the petal (see 3). Take the damp artist's brush and pull it from the outside edge to the centre of the flowers so that the two pink colours blend together. Repeat for all the rose petals, cleaning your brush from time to time.

9 To pipe the centres: take the yellow icing and pipe little dots into the middle of each open rose (see 4). Let dry for an hour or two.

10 Place one tier at a time on a turntable and, using a piping bag filled with white soft-peak royal icing, pipe a border along bottom and top edge of each tier. Let dry.

11 Stick two 7.5cm/3 inch thick round cake boards together with a dab of royal icing. Do the same with two 15cm/6 inch thick round cake boards and two 23cm/9 inch thick round cake boards. These will form the cake separators.

12 Cover the sides of each separator with 30mm wide satin ribbon and fix with a pin.

13 Now assemble the whole cake. Mark 4 points in the middle of the bottom tier so that they form a 12.5cm/5 inch square. Stick 4 plastic dowels into the cake at these points and cut them to the right length as described on page 188.

14 Repeat for the second tier, positioning the dowels in the middle to form a 5cm/2 inch square.

15 Stick the 23cm/9 inch round separator in the centre of the iced 40cm/16 inch thick round cake board, using a dab of royal icing. Centre the 30cm/12 inch bottom tier on top.

16 Place the 15cm/6 inch round cake separator on the bottom tier so it covers the plastic dowels that are stuck inside the bottom tier.

17 Next, place the 23cm/9 inch middle tier on top, followed by the 7.5cm/3 inch round separator and finally the 15cm/6 inch top tier.

'makes me think of English rose gardens'

Dropping Daisies

Rather similar in concept to the earlier Pink Wedding Cake, this equally striking cake is made just that touch more playful by the addition of the white sugar bows and by the use of a refreshing mint green as the base colour.

FOR ABOUT 90 PORTIONS

500g stiff-peak royal icing
(see page 191)
yellow food colour
icing sugar for dusting
small amount of clear alcohol
(such as vodka) or water
250g white sugar paste
filled and iced cake as described
on pages 184–5

EQUIPMENT

metal piping nozzle Wilton 104/103
greaseproof paper
flower nail
paper piping bags (see page 193)
small rolling pin
fine artist's brush
small plastic board
small kitchen knife

1 Using white and yellow stiff-peak royal icing, paper piping bags and piping nozzles, pipe 120 sugar daisies as described on pages 194-5 in 3 different sizes. Let dry overnight.

2 Meanwhile, on a surface dusted with icing sugar, roll the white sugar paste out to a long strip and cut out two 2cm/¾ inch wide strips that are long enough to go around the sides of the cakes.

3 Brush the bottom edge of each tier with alcohol or water using an artist's brush, and stick the strips of paste around each tier (see 1). Make sure you start and finish in the centre of the same side.

4 To make the bows, roll a smaller piece of paste out on the small plastic board and cut out two strips 2cm/¾ inch wide and 12cm/5 inches in length.

5 Using a small kitchen knife, cut two 'V' shapes out of the middle of each strip opposite each other (see 2).

6 Brush the middle of each strip with a little bit of water or alcohol and bring both ends of each strip to the middle to form the bow (see 3).

7 Roll another small amount of paste out and cut out 2 pieces of about 1 x 2cm/½ x ¾ inch. Brush the middle of each bow with some water or alcohol and push one small piece of the cut-out paste into the centre of each bow.

8 Stick each bow on to the sides of each tier where the ends of the paste strips join together, fixing it in place with some water or alcohol. Open up the bow's loops slightly to give them shape.

9 Finally stick the daisies randomly along the top edge of each tier, using dabs of royal icing.

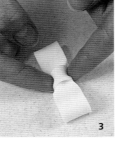

Romantic Rose Tower

Voluptuous roses in luscious pinks and gorgeous butterflies 'fluttering' at the end of curled wires turn this cake into a piece of pure romance. Inspired by A Midsummer Night's Dream, I designed this cake to create something different and unusual as a glamorous centrepiece for wedding receptions and birthday parties. It is very time-consuming to make, but is well worth the effort. You can make the roses a few weeks in advance, as they will keep well.

FOR 120 PARTY PORTIONS:

You need to do this at least 3 days ahead and make your marzipan roses and leaves at least 24 hours in advance to ensure they are dry.

4 (40 x 30cm/16 x 12 inch) sheets of Rich Dark Chocolate Cake (see pages 175-6)
500g Chocolate Ganache (see page 180)
icing sugar for dusting
2kg marzipan
2kg pink sugar paste
a little clear alcohol, such as vodka or gin
about 120 Marzipan Roses (see page 143) in different shades of pink
about 24 Marzipan Rose Leaves (page 199)
pink royal icing (page 191)

EQUIPMENT

about 10 round templates with diameters from 5cm to 30cm/2 to 12 inches for cutting out the cake layers
30cm/12 inch round cake board
large palette knife
large rolling pin
5mm/¼ inch guide sticks
small kitchen knife
pastry brush
paper piping bag (see page 193)
40cm + 45cm/16 + 18 inch round double cake board covered with pale pink sugar paste and deep pink ribbon (see page 186)
wired feather butterflies (see Suppliers, page 201)

1 Using your templates, cut out rounds of sponge with diameters graduated from 5cm to 30cm/2 inches to 12 inches.

2 Using a large palette knife, spread a little ganache on a 30cm/12 inch cake board and place the 30cm/12 inch sponge on top. Spread a thin layer of ganache over this first layer and place the next-largest sponge on top. Continue to assemble the cake layer by layer in this way to form a cone shape.

3 Cover the whole cake with chocolate ganache and smooth the surface. Place the cake in the fridge and leave it to set for at least 2 hours.

'this cake is pure romance'

4 Dust your working surface with icing sugar and roll out the marzipan to a thickness of 5mm/¼ inch, using your guide sticks. Make a paper template that will be big enough to form a cone, when rolled, that will cover the cake. Use this to mark and cut out a triangle of marzipan large enough to cover the cake.

5 Apply another thin coat of ganache to the cake.

6 Use your rolling pin to lift the marzipan triangle and carefully wrap it around the cake. Trim off excess top and the bottom. Leave it to harden overnight.

7 Next day, following the same procedure as with the marzipan, cover the cake with pink sugar paste, but instead of using chocolate ganache to stick it on, first brush the cake with the alcohol. Let the paste harden overnight.

8 Next day, pipe a dot of icing in the centre of the double cake board and place the cake on top.

9 Decorate the cake by sticking the marzipan roses and leaves on it with pink royal icing, starting at the bottom and working your way upwards (see 1 and 2 above).

10 Finally, stick the wired butterflies into the marzipan roses evenly over the cake, using larger butterflies at the bottom and smaller ones at the top.

11 When serving, make everyone aware that the wired butterflies are not edible, and make sure that they are removed before the cutting and eating of the cake.

American Sweet Heart

Romantically kitsch and sugary sweet, this cake of tiny little pink rosebuds and sugar heart motifs couldn't be more appealing and girly. As such, it is perfectly suited to something like a bridal shower party.

FOR ABOUT 70 PORTIONS
3 round cake tiers, 20cm/
    8 inches, 15cm/6 inches,
    10cm/4 inches in diameter,
    made from 3½ quantities of
    basic Victoria sponge,
    flavoured to choice (see
    page 174), covered with
    marzipan and then sugar paste
    coloured pastel pink for top
    and bottom tiers, and dark
    pink for the middle tier, each
    set on a matching thick cake
    board (see pages 134–6)
100g soft-peak royal icing
    see pages 191–2)
pink and green food colours
500g white sugar paste
icing sugar for dusting
edible glue or clear alcohol

EQUIPMENT
small plastic board
small rolling pin
small kitchen knife
paper piping bags (see page 193)
small palette knife
small bowl
pair of scissors
heart-shaped cookie cutter
    (about 5cm/2-inch diameter)
small brush
8 cake dowels
scribbler (Kit Box)
greaseproof paper
1.5 m pink satin ribbon,
    10mm width

Make and cover the three cakes at least 1 or 2 days ahead and trim the bases of the bottom and top tiers with ribbon, securing it in place with a little royal icing.

1 Adjust the scribbler to a measure of about 2.5cm/1 inch and carefully take it around the middle tier as shown (see 1, page 129) to mark the top limit of the icing border.

2 Divide the soft-peak royal icing into 3 and colour it 2 shades of pink and one green, then fill a piping bag with each colour. Place the middle cake tier on top of a piece of greaseproof paper and pipe a row of 2cm/¾-inch long stripes in alternating colours around the base (see 2, page 129). Finish each strip with a dot at the bottom and top. Let dry. Keep some of the green-coloured icing (covered) for later use.

3 Knead the white sugar paste until it is soft and pliable. Divide it in two and then mix each half with a different amount of pink food colour to produce two different shades of pink.

4 On a plastic board lightly dusted with icing sugar, roll out some of the pink paste to a long thin strip, trim the edges and cut it into small pieces of about 1x4cm/½ x 1½ inches. Roll each strip up into a little bud and let them dry (see 3–5). You will need about 250 dark-pink buds and 20 pale-pink buds.

5 Roll the remaining pale-pink paste out to about a thickness of about 2mm /¹⁄₁₂ inch and cut out heart shapes from it.

6 Lightly mark the bottom tier into 8 sections radially, like a wheel, and lightly brush the back of a heart with edible glue or clear alcohol (see 6), then stick it on to the cake at the outer part of each section (see 7).

7 Stick a row of dark-pink rosebuds around the outside of each heart, using little dabs of royal icing (see 8). Arrange the

pale-pink rosebuds individually over the middle tier and the remaining dark-pink buds in clusters of 3 all over the top tier.

8 Fill a piping bag with the remaining green icing. Cut the tip off in a V shape and pipe small leaves around the rosebuds (see 9). Let dry.

9 Assemble the cakes with 4 dowels each for the bottom and middle tiers, as described on page 187-8.

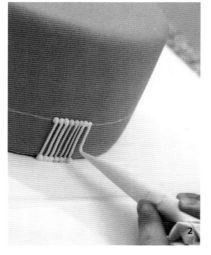

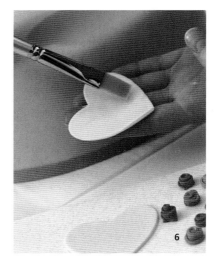

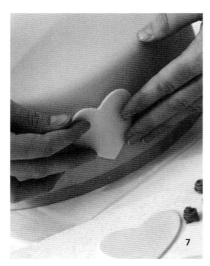

Butterfly Chocolate Cake

This clever and simple design is ideal for a not-so-traditional wedding. Chocolate brown combined with muted pastel colours is a very modish look right now. Some of my favourite pastels to use in this way are dusky pink, sage green or taupe.

FOR 120 PORTIONS

small amount of white vegetable fat

about 300g royal icing (see page 191)

dark-brown and blue food colours

3 round cake tiers 25cm/10 inches, 17.5cm/
   7 inches and 10cm/4 inches), made from 6
   quantities rich dark chocolate cake (see page
   175) layered with ganache (see page 180), iced
   with marzipan and dark-brown chocolate-
   flavoured sugar paste (see pages 184–5),
   assembled on a 35cm/14-inch round cake
   board covered in dark-brown chocolate-
   flavoured sugar paste (page 186)

EQUIPMENT

sheet of cellophane

small bowls

small palette knife

paper piping bags (see page 193)

pair of scissors

piece of thin cardboard

greaseproof paper

about 3 m chocolate-brown grosgrain ribbon,
   15mm width

metal pin

Make the butterflies 2 days ahead.

1 Rub a very thin layer of vegetable fat over a sheet of cellophane. Lay it on top of the butterfly template (see pages 206–7) and, using soft-peak (see page 192) chocolate-brown royal icing, pipe the outline of the wings (see 1). Let dry.

2 When dry, flood the wing centres with blue-coloured runny icing (see page 192 and 2–3) and let dry overnight.

3 Once the blue icing is completely dry, decorate the wings with small dots in soft-peak chocolate-brown icing. Let dry.

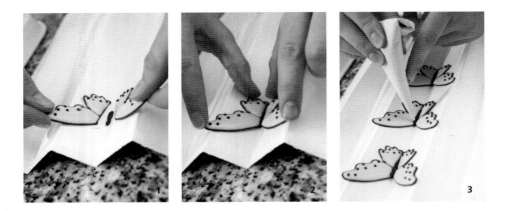

4 Fold a piece of cardboard to a V shape to support the wings when sticking them together and line it with a piece of greaseproof paper.

5 Pipe a short line of soft-peak chocolate-brown icing into the fold of the paper. Lift the wings off the cellophane and stick them into the brown icing (see 1 and 2). Pipe the body down the centre of the wings over the original brown icing (see 3). Let dry overnight.

TO DECORATE THE CAKE

6 Cut the ribbon into 4 pieces to cover the base of each tier and the cake board. Fix the ribbon around the board with a pin and the ribbon around the cake tiers with dabs of stiff-peak chocolate-brown icing (see page 192).

7 Using soft-peak blue royal icing, pipe small dots evenly around each side of the ribbon and around the edge of the cake board.

8 Arrange the butterflies all over the cake, fixing them in place with dabs of stiff chocolate-brown icing.

Brush-embroidered Daisy Cake

To create a vintage-style look here, I used a technique called 'brush embroidery' for which I painted the daisy design on the cake with a brush, using very lightly coloured royal icing.

FOR 70 PORTIONS

3 round cake tiers, 20cm/
   8 inches, 15cm/6 inches and
   10cm/4 inches in diameter,
   made from 3½ recipe
   quantities of basic Victoria
   sponge, flavoured to your
   choice (see page 174) and
   covered with marzipan
   (see page 185)
2kg ready-made ivory sugar paste
100g white sugar flower paste
small amount of white
   vegetable fat
cornflour for dusting
about 300g soft-peak royal icing
   (see pages 191–2)
yellow and green food colours

EQUIPMENT

large and small rolling pins
2 cake smoothers
daisy patchwork cutters
   (Marion Frost)
veined daisy plunger cutter (PME)
small non-stick plastic board
flower foam pad or celpad
stayfresh multi mat
celstick or cocktail stick
colour mixing palette
small bowls
palette knife
paper piping bags (see page 193)
pair of scissors
fine artist's brushes
8 cake dowels
5mm (¼-inch) marzipan spacers

Make and cover the cakes 1 or 2 days ahead.

EMBOSSING THE CAKE

1 Cover each cake with the ivory sugar paste as described on pages 184–5.

2 While the sugar paste is still soft, gently impress the daisy patchwork cutters into it to create the embossing (see 1 overleaf). Let the sugar paste dry overnight.

MAKING THE DAISY FLOWERS

3 In the meantime, make the daisy flowers. Mix the sugar flower paste with a small amount of white vegetable fat and knead it until it is smooth and pliable.

4 On a plastic board dusted with cornflour, roll out the paste until very thin. Using the daisy plunger cutter, cut out 5 daisies and place one flower at a time on the foam pad. Keep the others covered with the multi mat.

5 Roll the cel stick or cocktail stick over each petal to stretch it. Then carefully lay it over the well of a colour mixing palette and push the middle down with a small rolling pin (see 2). Let it dry. Repeat for the remaining daisies.

6 Once dry, colour some of the soft-peak royal icing yellow and pipe small dots into the flowers' centres. Reserve the rest of the yellow icing for later.

TO BRUSH-EMBROIDER THE CAKE

7 Divide the remaining icing in half and colour one half very pale green. Start with the green leaves. Pipe the outline using soft peak white icing for the outside and a very pale green soft-peak icing for the inside of the leaf shape. Take a fine artist's brush dampened with water and pull it from the outside to the middle of the leaf, which will create the leaf veins (see 3). Repeat with all the leaves, cleaning your brush from time to time.

8 When finished with the leaves, pipe the white outline for the daisy petals and again brush the icing from the outside edge towards the petal centre with a damp brush. Repeat for all the daisy petals, cleaning your brush from time to time. For the centres, pipe little dots of the yellow icing into the middle of each daisy.

9 Once the icing is dry, assemble the cakes with 4 dowels between each tier as described on page 187.

10 With the remaining white icing, pipe small dots with a 1cm/¼-inch gap between them around the base of each tier.

11 Arrange the daisies on top of the cake, fixing them in place with a dab of icing.

Bed of Roses

I was commissioned to create a 3-foot square version of this amazing cake for a wedding. It was a big challenge, as I had to make over 1,500 roses to cover such a huge area. After days of making roses, I finally delivered the cake to the venue, utterly exhausted, with swollen hands and covered in glitter. But I was really proud of my achievement. The Bed of Roses made an enormous impact and everyone who saw it was stunned. Since then, it has become one of my best-selling creations and deserves a place in this book as one of the most romantic cakes I have ever designed.

FOR ABOUT 40–60 PORTIONS
900g red sugar paste
small amount of royal icing
    (see page 191)
about 2kg marzipan
red food colour
icing sugar for dusting
magenta Hologram Glitter
    Sparkle (EdAble Art)
one 20cm/8-inch square single
    layer sponge cake, using
    1 recipe quantity of basic
    Victoria sponge mixture,
    flavoured to your choice
    (see page 174), covered
    with red marzipan (see
    pages 184–5)

EQUIPMENT
25cm/12-inch square cake board
About 1.2 m fuchsia-pink ribbon,
    15mm width
metal pin
small palette knife
paper piping bag (see page 193)
pair of scissors
cling film
2 sheets of cellophane

Prepare the cake board 2 or 3 days in advance and make your roses at least one day ahead.

1 Cover the cake board with the red sugar paste and decorate the sides with fuchsia ribbon as described on page 186.

2 Spread a thin layer of royal icing in the middle of the iced cake board and place the cake on top. Let dry.

3 Colour the marzipan deep red. Keep it covered in cling film to prevent it drying out.

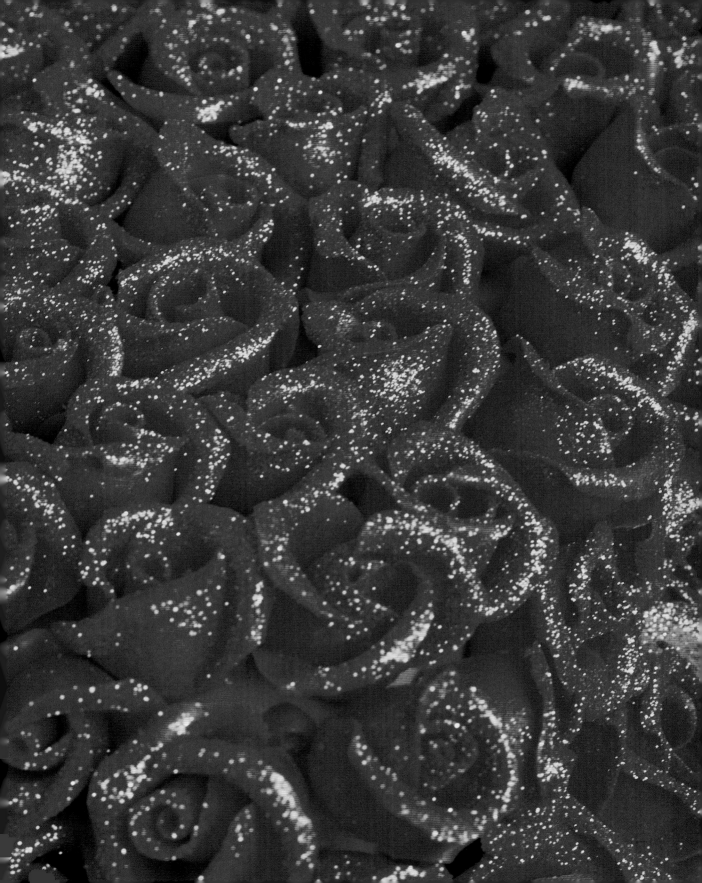

TO MAKE THE ROSEBUDS

(The number of roses you need to cover this cake depends on the size of your roses. You will also need a rosebud as the heart of each larger rose. For the cake illustrated, I used about 80 small rosebuds and about 20 larger open roses.)

4 For each rosebud, you need 3 hazelnut-sized balls of marzipan and one twice as large.

5 Place these pieces of marzipan between two sheets of cellophane (see 1) and start with the larger one by pushing it down sideways to make it longer, and then flatten one long side with your thumb until it is very thin (see 2). Dusting the marzipan with icing sugar helps prevent it sticking.

6 For the other 2 petals, begin to push one of the smaller balls down with your thumb, starting from the centre to one side, until it forms a round petal, with one thick and one thin side. Repeat with the other balls.

7 Take the large petal first and roll it into a spiral shape, thin side up (see 3). This will form the centre of the rose.

8 Take one of the smaller petals, thin side up, and lay it around the centre over the seam (see 4).

9 Then tuck the third petal slightly inside the second petal and squeeze it around the centre (see 5).

10 Slightly curve the edge of the petals out with your fingertips (see 6).

TO MAKE THE LARGER OPEN ROSES

11 To make each large open rose, continue by laying another 3 petals of the same size around a rosebud, each slightly overlapping the other. (see 7).

12 Again, slightly curve the edge of the petals outs with your fingertips to make larger roses.

13 Continue by laying another 5 petals of the same size around the rosebud, each slightly overlapping the other.

14 Slightly curve the edge of the petals out with your fingertips.

15 Pinch excess marzipan off the bottom of each rose (see 8). To finish the decorations

16 While still wet, dip the finished roses into the glitter sparkle (see 9), then let the roses dry overnight.

17 Once dry, stick the roses on the cake with red icing, first arranging the large roses around the sides and then putting the small buds all over the top.

1

2

3

4

5

6

7

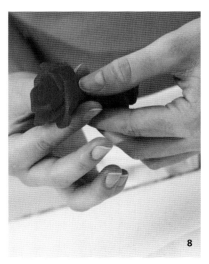

8

9

My Fair Lady Cake

As the name suggests, the inspiration for this cake comes from the famous Ascot scene designed by Cecil Beaton for the musical My Fair Lady. Black and white is currently much in vogue for urban weddings, so this cake design is proving very popular.

FOR 70 PORTIONS
500g sugar flower paste
small amount of wh te
    vegetable fat
cornflour for dusting
edible glue
small amount of royal icing
    (see page 191)
black food colour
icing sugar for dusting
3 round cake tiers, 20cm/
    8 inches, 15cm/6 inches and
    10cm/4 inches in diameter,
    made from 3½ recipe
    quantities of basic Victoria
    sponge, flavoured to your
    choice (see page 174), iced
    with marzipan and white
    sugar paste (see pages 184–5)
1 kg white sugar paste

EQUIPMENT
small non-stick plastic board
small rolling pin
cling film
large and medium rose petal cutter
    (FMM)
flower foam pad
stayfresh multi mat
bone tool and veining tool (JEM)
small colour palette
small palette knife
paper piping bags (see page 193)
kitchen knife
ruler
small pastry brush
8 cake dowels
strong pair of scissors

Make your flowers at least a day ahead. You will need about 28.

1 Knead the sugar flower paste with a small amount of vegetable fat until smooth and pliable.

2 On the plastic board lightly dusted with cornflour, roll out a small amount of flower paste very thinly, keeping the rest covered with cling film so it doesn't dry out.

3 First, cut out a large shape using the large rose petal cutter and place it on the foam pad.

4 Run the thick end of the bone tool along the edges until they become thin and slightly frilly. Then roll the veining tool across each petal.

5 Place the flower in the well of a cornflour-dusted painter's palette. Push the middle down with the end of the rolling pin and let dry. Repeat for all 28 flowers. Let dry.

6 Once these are dry, repeat steps 2 to 4 using the medium rose petal cutter and place on top of the larger dry ones. Fix the flower centres in place with edible glue. Let dry.

7 Once these are dry, pipe small dots of black royal icing into the flower centres.

COVERING THE CAKES WITH STRIPES

8 Knead the sugar paste until smooth and pliable. Divide in half and colour one piece deep black. Cover with cling film and let rest for about 1 hour.

9 On a clean surface dusted with icing sugar, roll out one piece of white and one piece of black sugar paste, both of the same size and about 3mm/⅛ inch thick. Trim the edges and cut each piece into strips of about 4x10cm/1½x4 inches).

10 Stick the strips on the side of each cake in alternating colours (see 1), using edible glue to fix them in place. Trim any excess paste off the top, using a kitchen knife (see 2) and push them flat on the sides using a cake smoother (see 3). Let dry.

11 Once these are dry, assemble the tiers, using the dowels and the instructions on page 187, as well as the dowel template on page 208, to support the tiers.

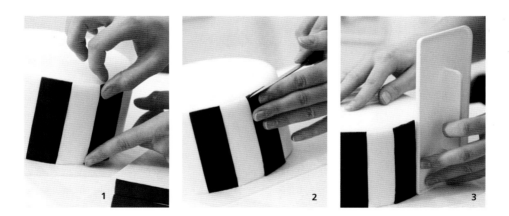

Neapolitan Monogrammed Cake

Use this very graphic and contemporary design to make your own signature cake by incorporating the initials of the bride and groom. Chocolate-brown and cream combine well with any pastel colour, such as blue, sage green or caramel.

FOR ABOUT 225 PORTIONS

about 2kg dark-brown chocolate-flavoured sugar paste

icing sugar for dusting

2 round cake tiers, 10cm/ 4 inches and 35cm/14 inches in diameter, made from 9 recipe quantities of basic Victoria sponge, flavoured to your choice (see page 174), covered with marzipan and then with sugar paste that has been coloured pastel pink (see page 185)

one 17.5cm/7-inch round cake tier, made from 1½ recipe quantities of basic Victoria sponge, flavoured to your choice (see page 174), covered with marzipan and then with sugar paste that has been coloured ivory (see page 185)

one 25cm /10-inch round cake tier, made from 4 recipe quantities of basic Victoria sponge, flavoured to your choice (see page 174), covered with marzipan and then with dark brown chocolate-flavoured sugar paste (see page 186)

edible glue or alcohol

about 300g royal icing (see page 191)

ivory, pink and dark-brown food colours

about 150g pastel-pink sugar paste

EQUIPMENT

45cm (18-inch) round thick cake board

small palette knife

small non-stick plastic board

small rolling pin

round pastry cutters (3cm and 5cm)

small bowls

paper piping bags (see page 193)

pair of scissors

cling film

small brush

tilting turntable

14 plastic cake dowels

pair of strong scissors

2.5 m chocolate-brown satin ribbon, 7mm width

1.5 m chocolate-brown satin ribbon, 15mm width

60cm ivory satin ribbon, 7mm width

metal pin

Make and cover the cake tiers at least 1 or 2 days ahead.

1 Cover the cake board with about 1.5kg dark-brown chocolate-flavoured sugar paste. Let dry overnight.

2 Spread a thin layer of royal icing into the middle of the iced cake board and place the largest tier on top of it.

3 On a plastic board dusted with icing sugar, roll out the rest of the brown sugar paste thinly and cut out circles using a 3cm round cutter. Stick them evenly spaced around the sides of the largest tier, using edible glue or alcohol to fix them in place.

4 Using soft-peak ivory royal icing (see page 191–2), pipe a row of tiny dots around each circle, then pipe another row of dots between every other one of the first row.

5 For the 17.5cm/7-inch ivory cake, repeat the same process using pastel-pink sugar paste, a 5cm round cutter and brown icing for piping the dots. Let dry before piping on the monograms.

6 To pipe the monograms, place the cake on top of a turntable slightly tilted away from you. Using brown soft-peak royal icing, write the monograms into the middle of the pink circles.

7 Place the 25cm/10-inch brown cake on top of the turntable. Mark the side of the cake evenly into sections about 5cm wide with tiny dots of icing. Slightly tilt the turntable away from you. With a piping bag filled with pink soft-peak icing, pipe a drape from one mark to another, turning the cake as required.

8 Now pipe 3 small loops above each join and finish the design with little piped dots.

9 Repeat steps 7 and 8 for the pink top tier cake using dark-brown icing.

10 Push 6 dowels into the bottom tier and 4 dowels each into the 25 cm/10-inch and 17.5cm/7-inch cakes, using the dowel template on page 208, and assemble the cake following the instructions on page 184–5.

11 Arrange the ribbons around the base of each tier, fixing the ends with icing and around the cake board, fixing the ends with a metal pin.

White Blossom Abundance

This design is ideal for beginners, as the sides of the cake are completely covered with flowers, so any little cracks in the icing can be perfectly hidden. You do need good piping skills to make the sugar flowers, but you can make them out of flower paste instead, using a simple five-petal flower cutter to achieve a very similar look.

FOR ABOUT 200 PORTIONS
about 1kg royal icing
   (see page 191)
ivory food colour
4 round cake tiers, 30cm/12
   inches, 25cm/10 inches,
   20cm/8 inches and 15cm/
   6 inches in diameter, made
   from 13½ recipe quantities
   of basic Victoria sponge,
   flavoured to your choice (see
   page 174), covered with
   marzipan and then with ivory
   sugar paste (see pages
   184-5)
35cm/14 inch round cake board
   covered with ivory sugar paste
   (see page 186)

EQUIPMENT
greaseproof paper
paper piping bags (see page 193)
pair of scissors
selection of petal piping tubes
   (I use Wilton 102, 103 and 104)
flower nail
small palette knife
small bowl
14 plastic cake dowels
pair of strong scissors or small saw
10cm/4-inch, 15cm/6-inch,
   20cm/8-inch and 25cm/10-inch
   round thick cake boards
2.5m ivory satin ribbon,
   15mm width
cling film or damp cloth
5 metal pins

Make the flowers 1 or 2 days ahead. The number of flowers you will need depends on how large you pipe them. I used about 300 flowers in three different sizes for this cake.

1 From a sheet of greaseproof paper, cut small squares slightly larger than the flower you want to pipe.

2 Make a paper piping bag and snip the tip off the empty bag to produce an opening large enough to fit a metal piping tube. Drop a Wilton 104 or PME 58R piping nozzle inside the bag, narrow end first.

3 Fill the bag with stiff-peak plain white royal icing (see pages 191–2).

4 Pipe a small dot of icing on top of the flower nail, stick one of the paper squares on top and hold the nail in one hand.

5 Hold the piping bag in the other hand at a 45-degree angle to the nail, with the wide end touching the centre of the flower nail and the narrow end pointing out and slightly raised.

6 Squeeze out the first petal and give the nail a one-fifth turn as you move the nozzle out towards the edge of the flower nail. Use less pressure as you are moving back towards the centre and curve the nozzle slightly to give the petal a natural shape. Stop squeezing as the wide end touches the centre of the nail and lift up the nozzle.

7 Repeat this 4 more times to make all the petals.

8 Remove the flower with its base paper from the nail and leave it to dry.

9 Colour some icing ivory and pipe small ivory dots into the centres as stamens.

10 Let the flowers dry in a warm place overnight. To decorate the cake

11 Once all the flowers are dry, stick them around the sides of each tier with dabs of royal icing. Mix the different sizes and use the smallest flowers to fill the gaps. Let dry.

12 Push 6 dowels into the largest cake and 4 dowels each into the 25cm/10-inch and 20cm/8-inch cake, using the dowel template on page 208 and the instructions on page 188.

13 Cut the ribbon into 5 pieces long enough to cover the base board and separator boards. Arrange them around each board and fix the ends with metal pins.

14 Stack the cakes on top of each other with a separator board in between each tier, starting with the largest cake board and cake at the bottom. Spread a small amount of royal icing between each tier and board to stabilise the construction.

Homage to Cath Kidston

I am a big fan of Cath Kidston's work and this wedding cake was inspired by some of her fabric and wallpaper designs. The mix of different patterns and cake shapes works particularly well, as I have tied them together by repeating colours and textures on every other tier. I have topped the cake with a crown of large handcrafted roses in luscious red with cerise-pink centres, which you can make well in advance.

FOR 320 PORTIONS

about 1.5kg ready-made pastel-pink sugar paste
about 250g sugar flower paste
red, pink and green food colours
ruby blossom tint dusting colour (Sugar Flair)
small amount of white vegetable fat
about 1kg royal icing (see page 191)
2 cake tiers, 35cm/14 inches and 25cm/10 inches square, made from 12½ recipe quantities of basic Victoria sponge, flavoured to your choice (see page 174), both covered with marzipan and then ivory and pastel-pink sugar paste respectively (see pages 184–5)
2 round cake tiers, 17.5cm/7 inches and 10cm/4 inches, made from 2 recipe quantities of basic Victoria sponge, flavoured to your choice (see page 191), both covered with marzipan and then ivory and pastel-pink sugar paste respectively (see pages 184–5)
edible glue
cornflour for dusting

EQUIPMENT

two 45cm/18-inch square thick cake boards stuck together with royal icing
cake smoother
selection of fine artist's brushes
rolling pin
rose petal cutter set
rose leaf cutters
rose leaf veining mat
calyx cutters, large and small
small non-stick plastic board
stayfresh multi mat
flower foam pad
small rolling pin
bone tool
sheets of cellophane
paper piping bags (see page 193)
2.5m ivory satin ribbon, 15mm width, for the 35cm/14-inch, 17.5cm/7-inch and 10cm/4-inch cake tiers
tilting turntable
1.85 m pink microdot ribbon, 25mm width, for the 45cm/18-inch square cake board
metal pin
19 cake dowels

Cover the double cake board and make the roses about 2 days ahead.

1 Cover the double cake board with pastel-pink sugar paste as described on page 186. Let dry.

2 Using cerise-pink sugar flower paste for the centres and deep red for the outer petals, make about 6 large open roses, 5 small rosebuds and a couple of green leaves as described on pages 197–9. Dust and steam the finished roses with ruby blossom tint as described on page 199.

Make the rose runouts the day before.

3 Place some cellophane, very thinly greased with vegetable fat, over the template. Using a paper icing bag of red soft-peak royal icing, trace the outlines of the petals and do the same with the leaves using green icing (see 1). Repeat piping the outlines of the template 4 times, one for each side. Let dry.

4 Once the outlines have dried, flood the centres of the roses with runny pink and red icing, and the leaves with 2 shades of green icing (see 2 and 3). Let dry overnight.

DECORATE THE PINK CAKE TIERS

5 Arrange ribbon around the base of the 10cm/4-inch top tier, held in place with a dab of icing, and pipe small ivory dots all over it. Let dry.

6 Place the 25cc/10-inch tier on top of the turntable, slightly tilted away from you. Using ivory soft-peak icing, pipe thin lines evenly from the top edge down to the bottom of the cake. You can use a smaller square cake board to act as a guide as shown. Let dry.

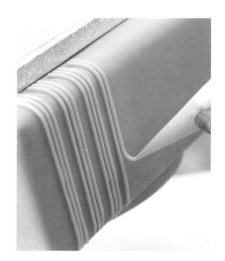

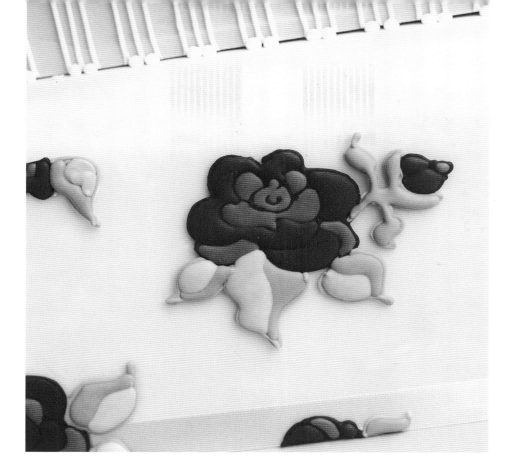

TO ASSEMBLE AND FINISH

7 Arrange the pink microdot ribbon around the side of the 45cm/18-inch double cake board and fix the ends with a metal pin at the back.

8 Spread a thin layer of icing into the middle of the base board and carefully put the 35cm/14-inch bottom tier in place. Cut a piece of ivory satin ribbon long enough to cover the sides of the cake and lay it around the base. Fix the ends with a small dab of icing. Arrange the rose runouts for the bottom tier all around the sides, fixing them in place with icing.

9 Arrange another piece of ivory satin ribbon around the base of the 17.5cm/7-inch ivory cake and stick on the little rose runouts with icing.

10 To assemble the cake, use 9 dowels for the bottom tier and 5 each for the second and third, as described on page 187 and using the dowel template on page 208.

11 Once the cake tiers have been stacked on top of one another, arrange the roses and leaves on the top tier, using stiff royal icing to fix them in place.

Something Borrowed, Something Blue...

We normally think of accessories when it comes to this famous tradition. But why not reflect something borrowed and something blue on the cake by using some old family jewellery and blue satin bows?

FOR 250 PORTIONS

small amount of royal icing (see page 191)
ivory food colour
4 round cake tiers, 35cm/14 inches, 27.5cm/11 inches, 20cm/8 inches and 12.5cm/5 inches, made from 16 quantities of basic Victoria sponge, flavoured to your choice (see page 174), iced with marzipan and ivory sugar paste, assembled on a 35cm/18-inch double round cake board covered with ivory sugar paste (see pages 184–7) and 60cm ivory satin ribbon
icing sugar for dusting
100g white sugar paste
white pearl lustre powder
edible glue or clear alcohol

EQUIPMENT

12 plastic dowels
small bowls
small palette knife
paper piping bag (see page 193)
about 3m blue satin ribbon, 70mm width
2 pieces of jewellery such as brooches, ideally heirlooms
pair of scissors
small non-stick plastic board
small rolling pin
textured rolling pin–scroll pattern (JEM)
stephanotis cutter
fine artist's brush

Make and cover your cakes at least 1 or 2 days ahead.

1 Once the tiers are assembled, using ivory soft-peak (see page 192) royal icing, pipe a dotted border around the base of the bottom and the third tier. Tie a blue ribbon bow around the second and the fourth tier and attach a piece of jewellery on to the middle of each bow. Trim the ribbon ends with scissors.

2 On a plastic board dusted with icing sugar, thinly roll out the sugar paste. Use the textured rolling pin to push a scroll design into the paste. Cut out about 20 stephanotis flower shapes and dust with white pearl lustre. Carefully turn them upside down and brush the backs thinly with edible glue or alcohol. Arrange in clusters cascading down the cake. Repeat until you have enough flowers to cover the cake (about 120).

3 Pipe small dots of ivory-coloured royal icing into the middle of the flowers.

Rosy Posy

Luscious pinks and purples are one of my favourite colour combinations – perfect for autumn weddings. The beauty of this cake is that you can tie it in with the reception by matching the colour of the roses to the ones in your bouquet.

FOR 100 PORTIONS

about 300g sugar flower paste
small amount of white vegetable fat
pink, purple and green food colours
plum blossom tint dusting colour (Sugar Flair)
edible glue
about 200g sugar paste
about 1 teaspoon gum tragacanth
3 round cake tiers, 25cm/10 inches, 17.5cm/
    7 inches), 10cm/4 inches in diameter, made
    from 6 recipe quantities of basic Victoria sponge,
    flavoured to your choice (see page 174), iced
    with marzipan and white sugar paste, assembled
    on a 35cm (14-inch) round cake board covered
    with white sugar paste (see page 184–7)
icing sugar for dusting
small amount of royal icing (see page 191)

EQUIPMENT

8 cake dowels
cling film
3.2m lilac grosgrain ribbon, 25mm width
rose petal cutter set
cocktail sticks
fine artist's brush
cake smoother
small non-stick plastic board
small rolling pin
rose leaf cutters
rose leaf veining mat
paper piping bag (see page 193)
pair of scissors

Make your roses at least 2 days ahead.

1 Knead the sugar flower paste with a small amount of white vegetable fat until smooth and pliable, then divide it into 3 equal pieces. Colour one piece of paste deep cerise pink, one lilac (a lighter purple) and one deep purple. Keep them covered with cling film until later use.

2 For this cake I made one large open rose, 3 open roses and 3 rosebuds (see pages 197–9), plus some extra rose petals. Dust the petals with the plum dusting colour and steam them (see page 199). Finish off with the calyxes, gluing them in place. Let dry.

TO MAKE THE STEMS

3 Knead the sugar paste until smooth and pliable. Add some green food colour and the gum tragacanth, and mix until the paste feels slightly stretchy. Cover with cling film and let it rest for about 1 hour.

4 In the meantime, arrange the ribbon around the bottom of each tier of the cake as shown.

5 To make the stems, roll little thin sausages out of the green sugar paste, using the cake smoother. Cut them into different lengths and stick them on the sides of the cake with the edible glue.

TO MAKE THE ROSE LEAVES AND FINISH THE CAKE

6 On a plastic board lightly dusted with icing sugar, roll the remaining green paste out until very thin. Cut out different sizes of rose leaves, push them between the veiner and attach them to the stems with edible glue or royal icing.

7 Now fix the rose heads and buds at the top of the endings of the stems with a dab of royal icing. If necessary, support them with your finger until the icing sets and use cocktail sticks to hold them in place. Arrange some petals down the sides of he cake.

Basics

Basic Equipment

1 large rolling pin
2 small non-stick plastic board
3 flower foam pad
4 marzipan spacers
5 design wheeler
6 artists' paint brushes
7 frilling or bulbous cone tool
8 ruler
9 scissors
10 dowelling template
11 small kitchen knife
12 small and large palette knife
13 large serrated kitchen knife
14 round pastry cutters
15 wire cooling rack
16 assortment of cake boards
17 whisk
18 rubber spatula
19 plastic sleeves
20 pastry brush
21 greaseproof paper
22 cake tins
23 selection of food colours
24 muffin cases
25 paper piping bag
26 muffin tray
27 baking tray
28 metal top and side scraper
29 veining tool
30 truffle dipping fork

31 bone tool
32 scriber needle
33 ball tool
34 cutting wheel
35 small rolling pin
36 cake leveller
37 assortment of cookie cutters
38 plastic dowels
39 mixing bowl/electric mixer with paddle attachment
40 assorted ribbons
41 rubber cameo moulds
42 sugar pearls
43 profile foam sheet
44 small painter's palette
45 selection of sprinkling sugars
46 cake smoothers
47 flower cutter and veiner

Baking Cookies

The recipes for cookies and cakes that I have developed during the past couple of years produce results that not only taste delicious, but also have a very good texture, and – although light – are solid enough to provide an ideal base for decoration. It is important that you follow each recipe carefully, as baking requires time and patience. As important as it is to master the techniques, it is equally important to use only the best ingredients available, such as organic butter and eggs, real vanilla extract and high-quality preserves and liqueurs.

Sugar Cookies

MAKES ABOUT 25 MEDIUM-SIZE OR 12 LARGE COOKIES
baking temperature: 180°C, gas 4;
baking time: 6–10 minutes, depending on size

INGREDIENTS
200g unsalted soft butter
200g caster sugar
1 egg, lightly beaten
400g plain flour, plus more for dusting

EQUIPMENT
electric mixer with paddle attachment
cling-film
pair of marzipan spacers
large rolling pin
cookie cutters in appropriate shapes
small palette knife
baking tray
greaseproof paper
wire cooling rack

OPTIONAL FLAVOURS
for vanilla cookies, add seeds from 1 vanilla pod
for lemon cookies, add finely grated zest of 1 lemon
for orange cookies, add finely grated zest of 1 orange
for chocolate cookies, replace 50g of the plain flour with 50g cocoa powder

1 In the electric mixer with paddle attachment, cream the butter, sugar and chosen flavouring until well mixed and just becoming creamy in texture. Don't overwork, or the cookies will spread during baking.

2 Beat in the egg until well combined. Add the flour and mix on low speed until a dough forms (see 1). Gather it into a ball, wrap it in cling film and chill it for at least 1 hour.

3 Place the dough on a floured surface and knead it briefly. Using marzipan spacers, roll it out to an even thickness (see 2).

  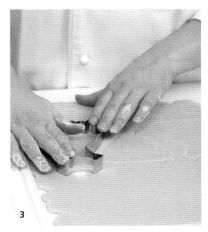

4 Use cookie cutters to cut out the desired shapes (see 3) and, using a palette knife, lay these on a baking tray lined with greaseproof paper. Chill again for about 30 minutes and preheat the oven to 180°C, gas 4.

5 Bake for 6–10 minutes. depending on size, until golden brown at the edges. Leave to cool on a wire rack. Wrapped in foil or cling film, they will keep well in a cool dry place for up to a month.

TIP: Always bake equally sized cookies together to make sure they cook in the same time. If you mix different sizes, the smaller ones are already cooked when the larger ones are still raw in the middle.

Gingerbread Cookies

MAKES ABOUT 40 MEDIUM-SIZE OR 20 LARGE COOKIES
baking temperature: 200°C, gas 6;
baking time: 8–12 minutes, depending on size

INGREDIENTS
250g cold salted butter, diced
1 teaspoon bicarbonate of soda
560g plain flour

FOR THE HOT MIX
5 tablespoons water
210g brown sugar
3 tablespoons treacle
3 tablespoons golden syrup
3 tablespoons ground ginger
3 tablespoons ground cinnamon
1 teaspoon ground cloves

EQUIPMENT
deep heavy saucepan
wooden spoon or plastic spatula
electric mixer with paddle attachment
sieve
cling film
pair of marzipan spacers
rolling pin
cookie cutters in appropriate shapes
small palette knife
baking tray
greaseproof paper
wire cooling rack

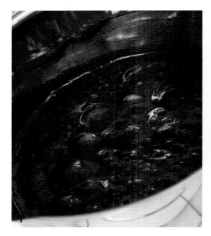

GINGERBREAD COOKIES (CONTINUED)

1 Place all the ingredients for the hot mix in a deep heavy saucepan and bring to the boil, stirring (see 1).

2 Once boiled, remove the pan from the heat and, using a wooden spoon or plastic spatula, carefully stir in the diced butter (see 2).

3 Once these are well combined, add the bicarbonate of soda and whisk the mix through briefly.

4 Pour into the bowl of the electric mixer and allow to cool until just slightly warm.

5 Once the mixture has cooled, sieve the flour over the top and start combining the two on a low speed, using the paddle attachment, until it forms a wet and sticky dough (see 3).

6 Wrap the dough in cling-film and chill for a couple of hours or overnight.

7 Place the chilled dough on a floured clean surface and knead it through briefly.

8 Place the kneaded dough between a pair of marzipan spacers and roll it out to an even thickness.

9 Use the cookie cutters to cut out the desired shapes and lay them on a baking tray lined with greaseproof paper.

10 Chill again for about 30 minutes. Preheat the oven to 200°C, gas 6.

11 Bake the cookies in the preheated oven for about 8-12 minutes, depending on the cookie size, until just firm to the touch.

12 Lift off the tray and allow to cool on a wire rack. Wrapped in foil or cling film, they will keep well in a cool dry place for up to a month.

TIPS

Cookie dough or uncooked cookies can be wrapped in cling-film and stored in the freezer for up to 3 months.

Cookies baked from frozen hold better in shape as they don't tend to spread as much as chilled ones.

Baked sugar cookies will keep for up to 1 month and gingerbread cookies up to 3 months, if kept in an airtight container or cookie jar.

Baking Cakes

While traditional Victoria sponge and rich dark chocolate cake are still the most popular choices for large cakes as well as cup cakes and fondant fancies, I have been finding there is increasing demand for more adventurous types of cake, such as the marble cake, because it looks so stunning when sliced open. I have also recently widened my repertoire of fillings so that my cakes are just as exciting to bite into as they are to look at.

Lining Cake Tins

EQUIPMENT
square or round cake tin of the
    required size
greaseproof paper
pair of scissors
pastry brush

1 Place the cake tin on top of the greaseproof paper, draw a line around the base with a pencil and use that as a guide to cut out a piece to line the base.

2 Then cut out a strip that is about 5cm wider than the depth of your tin and long enough to line the inside edge. Fold 2.5cm of this strip over along its length and cut little snips along the folded edge up to the crease.

3 Place the long paper strip with the snipped edge at the bottom inside the tin to cover the sides (see 1).

4 Now place the paper base on top and make sure the snips and the base are forming a sharp corner and won't allow any dough to leak through the paper lining (see 2). For square tins, use the same technique as above, but fold the long strip that covers the sides at the four corners to fit neatly inside the tin (see 1).

1

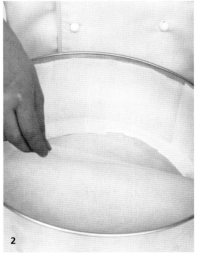

2

Victoria Sponge

MAKES ONE 20CM SPONGE CAKE (HALF A TIER), 25 FONDANT FANCIES OR 20-24 CUP CAKES

baking temperature: 180°C, gas 4; baking time: 12–15 minutes for cup cakes, 20–45 minutes for large cakes, depending on size

INGREDIENTS
200g salted butter, softened
200g caster sugar
4 medium eggs
200g self-raising flour
100ml sugar syrup (see page 178), flavoured to your choice

EQUIPMENT
electric mixer with a paddle attachment
mixing bowl
20cm/10-inch cake tin for large cake or fondant fancies, muffin trays and muffin cases for cup cakes
wooden skewer
greaseproof paper
large palette knife (for large cakes and fondant fancies)
small spoon or large plastic piping bag (for cup cakes)
wire cooling rack
pastry brush

For other sizes and quantities, please refer to the guide on page 202.

OPTIONAL FLAVOURS
For vanilla sponge, add the seeds of 1 vanilla pod
For lemon sponge, add the finely grated zest of 2 lemons
For orange sponge, add the finely grated zest of 2 oranges
For chocolate sponge, replace 50g of the flour with cocoa powder and add 50g melted dark chocolate to the butter and sugar mix

1 Preheat the oven to 180°C, gas 4.

2 Place the butter, sugar and chosen flavouring in an electric mixer and, using the paddle, cream together until pale and fluffy.

3 Beat the eggs lightly in another bowl and slowly add to the mix, while paddling on medium speed. If the mixture starts curdling, add a little bit of flour.

4 Once the eggs and the butter mixture are combined, mix in the flour at low speed.

5 Line the required baking tin as explained on the previous page. For cup cakes, place the paper cases into the muffin trays.

6 Spread the dough evenly into the tin using a palette knife (see 1 and 2).

TIP: As sponge always rises more in the centre, spread it slightly higher around the edge. For cup cakes, fill the paper cases about two-thirds full, using a small spoon or a plastic piping bag.

7 Bake for 12-15 minutes for cup cakes and 20-45 minutes for large cakes, depending on size. The sponge is cooked when it springs back to the touch and the sides are coming away from the tin. Alternatively, you can check it by inserting the tip of a clean thin knife into the centre; it should come out clean.

8 Once the sponge is baked, let it rest for about 15 minutes.

9 Prick the top of the sponge with a wooden skewer and, using a pastry brush, soak it with the syrup, while the sponge is still warm.

10 For cup cakes, wait about 10 minutes after baking before soaking the cup cakes with the sugar syrup. This way they will absorb the syrup immediately and not seem dry.

11 Once cool, remove the cake from the tin and cool on a wire rack.

12 For large cakes, once cool, wrap the sponge in greaseproof paper and then foil, then store in a cool dry place overnight. I prefer to let sponges rest overnight as they tend to crumble if cut, layered and iced on the same day as baking.

13 Sponges and cup cakes have a shelf-life of up to 7 days after icing, and are suitable for freezing. If wrapped well, they can be frozen for up to 1 month.

TIP: Bake cup cakes on the day they'll be iced, as they dry out fast.

Rich Dark Chocolate Cake

MAKES ONE 20CM CAKE OR 20–24 CUP CAKES
baking temperature: 160°C, gas 3; baking time: about 15 minutes for cup cakes, 25–45 minutes for large cakes, depending on size

INGREDIENTS
75g dark couverture chocolate drops
100ml milk
225g brown sugar
75g salted butter, softened
2 medium eggs, slightly beaten
150g plain flour
1½ tablespoons cocoa powder
½ teaspoon baking powder
½ teaspoon bicarbonate of soda

EQUIPMENT
20cm/10-inch cake tin for large cake
    or fondant fancies, muffin trays
    and cases for cup cakes
greaseproof paper
deep saucepan
electric mixer with a paddle
    attachment
sieve
mixing bowl
measuring jug
rubber spatula or wooden spoon

For other sizes and quantities, please refer to the guide on page 202. This cake is a little bit more moist than most other chocolate cake recipes, but it is also denser and slightly heavier at the same time, which makes it an excellent base for tiered cakes. It has a shelf-life of up to 10 days after icing.

1 Preheat the oven to 160°C, gas 3.

2 Line the required baking tin as described on page 173. For cup cakes place the muffin paper cases into the muffin trays.

3 Place the chocolate, milk and half the sugar in a deep span and bring to the boil, stirring occasionally.

4 Using an electric mixe with a paddle attachment, beat the butter and remaining sugar until pale and fluffy.

5 Slowly add the eggs.

6 Sift the flour, cocoa powder, baking powder and bicarbonate of soda and add to the mixture while mixing at a low speed.

7 While the chocolate mix is still hot, using a measuring jug, slowly pour it into the dough while mixing at low speed (see 1).

8 Once combined (see 2), pour the mix from the bowl directly into the lined tin (see 3). For cup cakes, first transfer the cake mix into a jug, as it is very liquid, and fill the cases about two-thirds full.

9 Bake for 15 minutes for cup cakes, 25–45 minutes for large cakes, depending on size. It is cooked when it springs back to the touch and the sides are coming away from the tin. Or, insert a clean kitchen knife into the centre; it should come out clean.

10 Once the cake is/cup cakes are baked, let it rest for about 15 minutes. Once cool, remove the cake(s) from the tin.

11 For storage, wrap in greaseproof paper and then in foil and store in a cool dry place overnight. I let sponges rest overnight as they tend to crumble if baked, cut, layered and iced on the same day. For cup cakes, I recommend baking on the same day they will be iced, as they tend to dry out faster. This cake is suitable for freezing. Wrapped well, it can be frozen for up to 3 months.

Marble Cake

MAKES ONE 20CM CAKE
Baking temperature 180°C, gas 4;
baking time: about 20-45 minutes

INGREDIENTS
FOR THE VANILLA MIX
100g salted butter, softened

100g caster sugar
2 medium eggs
100g self-raising flour

FOR THE CHOCOLATE MIX
100g salted butter, softened
100g caster sugar

2 medium eggs
70g self-raising flour
30g cocoa powder
pinch of baking powder

100ml vanilla sugar syrup
  (page 178)

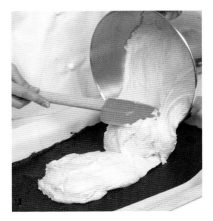

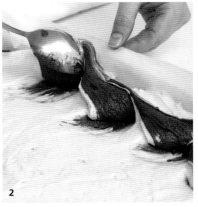

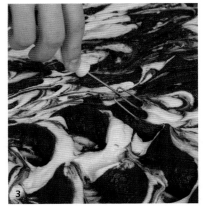

EQUIPMENT
baking tin in required size and shape
greaseproof paper
electric mixer with paddle attachment
sieve
bowls
rubber spatula or wooden spoon
tablespoon
fork or truffle dipping fork
pastry brush
wire cooling rack
kitchen knife

1 Line a baking tin with greaseproof paper as described on page 173.

2 Prepare the vanilla mix as for the Victoria sponge, page 174, steps 1–4.

3 For the chocolate mix, repeat Victoria sponge, steps 1–3, then sift the flour, cocoa powder and baking powder together, add it the batter and mix it together at a low speed.

4 Spread the mix into the lined tin first using a palette knife, then spread the vanilla mix on top (see 1).

5 With a tablespoon, fold through bit by bit (see 2), then run a fork through for marbling effect (see 3).

6 Bake for 20–45 minutes. Test if done with a clean knife inserted into the centre; it should come out clean.

7 Continue as for steps 8–12 of Victoria sponge.

Sugar Syrups

MAKES 100ML
Roughly the amount needed for a 20cm/8-inches layered cake tier, a 30cm/12-inches single tier square sponge to make 25 fondant fancies, or 20-24 cup cakes.

INGREDIENTS
FOR VANILLA SYRUP
5 tablespoons water
75g sugar
seeds from ½ vanilla pod or
    1 teaspoon Madagascan vanilla
    essence

FOR LEMON SYRUP
5 tablespoons freshly squeezed
    lemon juice
75g sugar
1 tablespoon Limoncello liqueur

FOR ORANGE SYRUP
5 tablespoons freshly squeezed
    orange juice
75g sugar
1 tablespoon Grand Marnier liqueur

EQUIPMENT
deep saucepan
spatula

1 Place the water or juice and sugar in a deep saucepan and bring to the boil. Remove from the heat and allow it to cool.

2 Once cool, stir in the flavourings.

3 Ideally, let the syrup infuse overnight as this will bring out the most of the flavours.

4 To store sugar syrup, keep it in an airtight bottle or container inside the fridge and it will last for up to 1 month.

Buttercream Frosting

MAKES 500G

Roughly the amount you will need to layer a 20cm/8-inch cake tier

INGREDIENTS

250g unsalted butter, softened
250g icing sugar, sifted
pinch of salt

OPTIONAL FLAVOURS

For vanilla buttercream (see 4), add the seeds of 1 vanilla pod
For lemon (see 3), add the finely grated zest of 2 lemons
For orange (see 1), add the finely grated zest of 2 oranges
For strawberry (see 2), add 2 tablespoons good strawberry jam and a tiny drop of pink food colour

For chocolate (see 5), replace half the buttercream with chocolate ganache (overleaf)
For mocha buttercream, add a double shot of cool espresso to the chocolate buttercream

EQUIPMENT

electric mixer with a paddle attachment

For other sizes and quantities please refer to the guide on page 202.

Following a traditional English recipe, I use equal quantities of butter and icing sugar to make my buttercream. The method is very simple and, as it is an egg-free recipe, it has a longer shelf-life than most other buttercreams.

1 Place the butter, icing sugar, salt and flavouring in the bowl of an electric mixer and, using the paddle attachment, bring the mixture together on low speed. Turn the speed up and beat until light and fluffy.

2 If not using it immediately, store in a sealed container in the fridge and bring it back to room temperature before use. It has a shelf-life of up to 2 weeks if refrigerated.

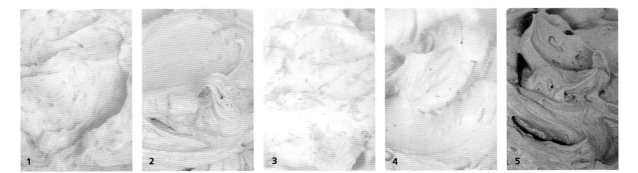

1   2   3   4   5

Belgian Chocolate Ganache

MAKES 1 KG
Roughly the amount you will need to layer a 20cm/8-inch cake tier

INGREDIENTS
500g dark couverture chocolate drops (minimum 53% cocoa content)
500ml single cream

EQUIPMENT
heatproof mixing bowl
saucepan
whisk

For other sizes and quantities please refer to the guide on page 202.

1

2

3

1 Place the chocolate drops in a bowl.

2 Place the cream in a saucepan, stir well and heat it up to a bare simmer.

3 Pour the hot cream over the chocolate (see 1) and whisk them together until smooth (see 2 and 3). Don't over-whisk the ganache, as it can split quite easily.

4 Cool slightly until just setting before use. It can be stored in a sealed container in the fridge for up to a month.

Layering and Icing Cakes

Tiered cakes, as well as miniature cakes, provide the option of mixing different flavours of cakes. If you would like to make a tiered cake with different flavours, you have to bear in mind that the bottom tier has to carry the weight of the other tiers and therefore a stronger cake base should be used for the bottom tiers and lighter cakes for the top. For example, if you use my recipes, I recommend using chocolate cake for the lower tiers and the lighter Victoria sponge-based cakes for the upper tiers. You will find a full portion guide and charts indicating amounts of basic cake mixtures, fillings and covering required for various types and sizes of cakes on page 202. A template for the positioning of dowels to support cake tiers is also given on page 208.

Miniature Cakes

MAKES 8-10 DESSERT-SIZED MINIATURE CAKES

I usually bake and layer miniature cakes 3 days in advance, ice them the next day and add the decoration the day before. The illustrations overleaf show a marble cake with buttercream filling, but they can be made with any cake or filling.

INGREDIENTS

30cm/12-inch square sponge cake (page 174)

FOR THE FILLING:

about 600g buttercream or ganache (page 179 or 175), flavoured to your choice

100ml sugar syrup (page 178), flavoured to your choice
about 4 heaped tablespoons jam, marmalade, lemon curd (optional)
small amount of icing sugar for dusting
1.5kg marzipan
1.5kg sugar paste
small amount of clear alcohol (I use vodka as it has a neutral taste) or water

EQUIPMENT

cake leveller or large serrated knife
small palette knife
thin cake cards to match the number, size and shape of your chosen miniature cakes
pastry brush
cling film
large rolling pin
7.5cm round high pastry cutter
icing sugar sieve
pair of marzipan spacers
small kitchen knife
pair of cake smoothers

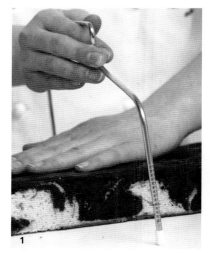

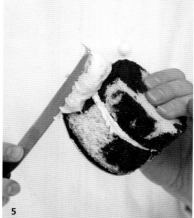

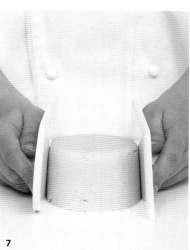

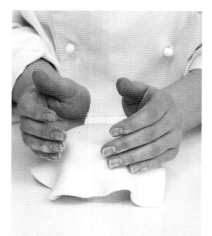

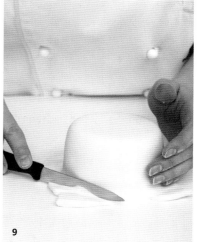

1 Using a cake leveller or large serrated knife, trim the top crust off your sponge (see 1).

2 Using the cutters, cut 16 rounds from the sheet of sponge (see 2).

3 Place half of them on the cake cards with a dab of buttercream or ganache and soak the tops with sugar syrup (see 3).

4 Using a small palette knife, spread them with a layer of filling of buttercream, ganache, jam, marmalade or ganache (see 4) and place the other sponges on top of them (see 5).

5 Again, soak the tops of the sponges with sugar syrup.

6 Cover each mini cake all around with buttercream or ganache and chill until set and feeling nice and firm.

7 Once set, on a smooth surface lightly dusted with icing sugar, roll out the marzipan using spacers to get an even thickness. Cut the marzipan into squares that are large enough to cover the cakes.

8 Cover one cake at a time with the marzipan and gently push it down the sides (see 6). Avoid tearing the edges. Trim off excess using the pastry cutter.

9 Polish the sides and tops of each cake with the cake smoothers (see 7).

10 Let the marzipan set for a few hours or preferably overnight.

11 Once the marzipan is set, brush each cake with a thin layer of clear alcohol.

12 Repeat steps 7 to 9 (see pics 8 and 9), using the sugar paste instead of marzipan. Let dry completely, preferably overnight.

MY FAVOURITE CAKE AND FILLING COMBINATIONS
- Vanilla sponge, soaked with vanilla syrup, layered with raspberry preserve and vanilla buttercream
- Lemon sponge, soaked with lemon and Limoncello syrup, layered with lemon curd and lemon buttercream
- Orange sponge, soaked with orange and Grand Marnier syrup, layered with luxury orange marmalade and orange buttercream
- Rich dark chocolate cake layered with Belgian chocolate ganache
- Vanilla sponge, soaked with morello cherry jam
- Rich dark chocolate cake layered with vanilla buttercream and mocha buttercream
- Lemon sponge layered with vanilla, strawberry and chocolate buttercream

Large Cakes

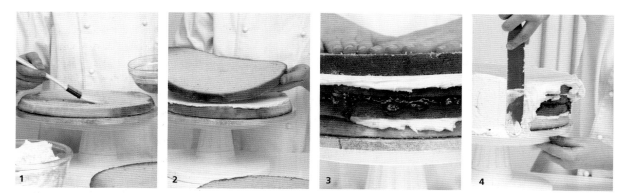

MAKES ONE 20CM ROUND CAKE TIER

For a 20cm/8-inch round cake tier you will need two 20cm/8-inch round sponges (see the quantities guide on page 202).

INGREDIENTS

about 600g buttercream or ganache, jam, marmalade or lemon curd
    (for Victoria sponge only)
about 200ml sugar syrup (for Victoria
    sponge and Marble cake only)
icing sugar for dusting
about 850g marzipan
small amount of clear alcohol (I use
    vodka as it has a neutral taste)
about 850g sugar paste

EQUIPMENT

cake leveller or large serrated knife
small kitchen knife
20cm round cake board
large palette knife
pastry brush
metal side scraper
turntable
icing sugar sieve
large rolling pin
pair of marzipan spacers
pair of cake smoothers
scriber

1 Using the leveller or serrated knife, trim the top and bottom crusts off both sponges.

2 Slice each sponge in half so you have 4 layers of the same depth (about 2cm each).

3 Place the cake board on the turntable and spread with a thin layer of buttercream or ganache. Put the first sponge layer on top and soak with sugar syrup if required (see 1).

4 Spread the sponge with buttercream or ganache, put the second layer on top (see 2). Soak with syrup.

5

6

7

8

5 Keep on layering the remaining pieces of sponge in this way with preserves or buttercream or ganache until all 4 layers are assembled. Press the layers down gently but firmly to ensure that the cake is level (see 3).

6 Using a large palette knife, coat the outside of the cake with buttercream or ganache (see 4). Start spreading from the top centre and towards the edge as you are rotating the turntable.

7 Push the buttercream down the sides and spread it evenly all around the sides.

8 Use a metal side scraper to clean up the sides (see 5) and do the same on the top with a palette knife.

9 Chill for at least 2 hours or overnight until the cake has set and feels firm.

10 Once set, dust a working surface with icing sugar, place marzipan on it and, using the marzipan spacers, roll out to an even round large enough to cover the top and sides.

11 Lift the marzipan with the rolling pin, lay it over the cake (see 6) and gently push it down the sides. Trim off any excess marzipan using the kitchen knife.

12 Polish the marzipan with the cake smoothers (see 7) and use the palms of your hands to smooth the edges. Let the marzipan dry, preferably overnight.

13 Once set, brush the marzipan with a thin coat of clear alcohol to stick on the sugar paste icing. The alcohol not only destroys any bacteria that may have built up while storing the cake, but it also evaporates within minutes after its application and therefore creates a strong and hygienic glue between the marzipan and the sugar paste. Should you prefer not to use alcohol, you can use boiled cold water instead.

14 Repeat steps 10 to 12 using sugar paste instead of marzipan (see 8).

TIPS: For tiered cakes, start the preparation about 5 to 6 days before the event. For example, if the wedding is on a Saturday, bake the sponges on the Monday before and layer them on the Tuesday. Cover the cakes with marzipan on Wednesday and leave overnight, so that the marzipan has time to dry. On Thursday, cover the cakes with sugar paste and let them set again overnight. This gives you the whole of Friday to apply your decorations, which you can prepare a couple of weeks in advance.

For single tiered cakes, start about 3 to 4 days before the event, as the cake can be covered with marzipan and sugar paste on the same day.

To make one cake tier you need two sponges of the same size. For a well-proportioned tiered cake, each tier should ideally be about 8.5cm high, including cake board, before applying the marzipan and icing.

Make sure that all tiers have the exact same height unless a mixture of different heights is intended.

Covering Cake Boards

INGREDIENTS
icing sugar for dusting
small amount of clear alcohol
sugar paste (see the quantity
    guide on page 202)

EQUIPMENT
thick cake board of the required size
pastry brush
rolling pin
cake smoother

small kitchen knife
15mm wide satin ribbon to cover
    the sides

1 Dust the cake board thinly with icing sugar and brush it with a little alcohol (to make a glue for the sugar paste).

2 Roll the sugar paste out to about 3mm thick and large enough to cover the cake board.

3 Use the rolling pin, lift the paste and lay it over the board (see 1).

4 Let the cake smoother glide carefully over the surface of the paste and push out any air bubbles.

5 Lift the board with one hand and push the paste down the side with the smoother in the other hand (see 2).

6 Trim the excess paste off with a sharp kitchen knife (see 3) and let the sugar paste dry for 1 to 2 days.

7 Once the paste is dry, wind the ribbon around the edge of the board and fix the ends with double-sided sticky tape.

Assembling Tiered Cakes

INGREDIENTS

cake tiers of different sizes,
   covered with marzipan and
   sugar paste
iced cake board about 7.5–10cm
   larger than the bottom tier
royal icing (see page 191)
small amount of sugar paste the
   same colour as the icing
small amount of water

EQUIPMENT

plastic dowels (4 for each tier
   except the top one)
palette knife
serrated kitchen knife
pair of strong scissors
food colour pen
dowel template (page 208)
paper piping bag (page 193)
small bowl
damp cloth
spirit level
pair of tweezers

1 Using a palette knife, spread the centre of the iced board with a thin layer of royal icing that doesn't exceed the size of the bottom tier.

2 Carefully lift your bottom tier with the palette knife and centre it on top of the cake board (see 1).

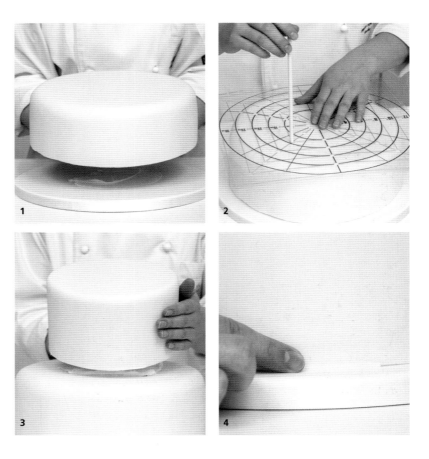

3 Using the template, mark positions for 4 dowels and push dowels down into the cake (see 2, previous page). (They stop upper tiers sinking into lower ones.)

4 With a food colour pen, mark each dowel about 1mm above the point at which it comes out of the cake.

5 Carefully remove the dowels, line them up next to one another and cut to the same length, using the average mark as a guide line. Stick them back in the cake. To see if they all have the same height, place a cake board on top of them and check that it sits straight, ideally using a small spirit level. Should you have to readjust the length of a dowel, carefully pull it out of the cake with tweezers and trim it with scissors then replace.

6 Once happy with the dowels, spread a little icing in the middle of the cake, carefully lift the second tier with your palette knife and centre it on top of the bottom tier.

7 Repeat steps 3 to 6 for second and third tiers if required.

8 Once all your tiers are assembled, mix the sugar paste with water to a thick but smooth paste. Put in a paper piping bag and squeeze into the gaps between tiers to fill them.

9 Dampen your finger with a damp cloth and run it along the filled gaps to wipe off excess paste.

TIP: Depending on transportation and distance to the event, it may be safer to assemble a tiered cake on site.

Dipping Fondant Fancies

Liquid fondant is widely used as a filling for chocolate truffles, etc., or as a glaze for pastries. It has a very long shelf-life and tastes deliciously smooth when flavoured with fruit juices, essences or liqueurs. As it is white, it provides an ideal base for mixing brilliant colours. Made by boiling together sugar, glucose syrup and water, it requires experience and skill to achieve the right consistency. To keep it simple, I use ready-made fondant.

MAKES 25 FONDANT FANCIES
INGREDIENTS
20cm/8-inch square Victoria sponge, well soaked with syrup (page 178), trimmed and layered with the filling of your choice (pages 184-5)
1 heaped tablespoon sieved apricot jam
icing sugar for dusting
about 150g marzipan
about 1kg ready-made liquid fondant

small amount of liquid glucose
selection of liquid food colours (optional)

EQUIPMENT
tray
cling film
pastry brush
large rolling pin
small knife
microwave cooker
small microwaveable bowls

truffle fork
wire cooling rack
25 silver muffin cases (optional)

1 Wrap your layered sponge cake well in cling film and chill it for at least an hour or so, to give it time to firm up.

2 Once it is cool and firm, warm the apricot jam, unwrap the sponge and spread a thin layer of jam over the top, using the pastry brush.

3 On a work surface lightly dusted with icing sugar, knead the marzipan until smooth and pliable. Shape it into a ball and roll it out to a square large enough to cover the top of the sponge and about 3mm thick.

4 Carefully lift it and lay it over the top of the cake. Trim the excess, if necessary.

5 Slice the marzipan-topped sponge into 4cm squares and spread the tops with a thin layer of jam (see 1).

6 Put the fondant in a large microwaveable bowl and gently heat it in the microwave cooker at medium heat for about 1 minute. Stir in the glucose and heat it again for about 20 seconds at a time, until it is warm and runny. (Alternatively, heat it in a saucepan over very low heat, stirring. Do not allow the fondant to boil, or it will lose its shine when cool again.) If necessary, you can add a little sugar syrup to it to make it more liquid (you looking for a thick pouring consistency).

7 If you would like to mix the fondant with different colours, divide it between some bowls and add a few drops of food colour at a time until you achieve the desired shades.

8 Dip one cake at a time upside down into the fondant (see 2), until about three-quarters of the sides are covered. To lift out, hold with two fingers at the bottom and a truffle fork at the top (see 3), ensuring you don't push the fork into the marzipan as it may tear it off. Quickly shake off excess icing and place the cake on the cooling rack (see 4). Leave it for the icing to set.

9 Carefully remove the fancies from the rack by cutting them loose at the bottom using a small kitchen knife and place in the paper cases. This is best done with slightly wet fingers, to prevent the icing sticking to them. Gently push the sides of the paper case against the sides of the cake and, as they stick, they take on the square shape. Place the cakes closely next to each other until ready for decoration. Again, this will help the paper cases stay square.

10 Iced fondant fancies keep for about 7 days in a cake box or wrapped in foil. Don't store them in the fridge or the icing will soften up.

Dipping Cup Cakes

MAKES 20–24

INGREDIENTS

2–3 heaped tablespoons sieved
  apricot jam
20–24 well-soaked cup cakes
  (pages 174–5)
About 1kg ready-made liquid fondant
small amount of plain sugar syrup
1 heaped teaspoon liquid glucose
selection of food colours

EQUIPMENT

pastry brush
microwave cooker
small microwaveable bowls
small palette knife

1 Warm the jam and brush a thin
layer over each cup cake to seal it
(see 1).

2 Put the fondant in a large
microwaveable bowl and gently heat
in the microwave cooker at medium
for 1 minute. Stir in the glucose and
heat again for 20 seconds at a time,
until warm and runny. (Or, heat in a
pan over very low heat, stirring. Do
not allow the fondant to boil, or it
will lose its shine.) If necessary, add
a little sugar syrup to make it more
liquid (you are looking for a thick
pouring consistency).

3 If you would like to mix the
fondant with different colours, divide
it between some bowls and add a
few drops of colour at a time until
you get the desired shades.

4 Dip all the cup cakes of one colour
first into the fondant (see 2), shake
off excess and let set before moving
on to the next colour. By the time
you have dipped the last cakes, the
icing of the first will have set and you
can begin with the second coat of
icing, as before. Dipping each cake
twice will ensure a beautifully smooth
and shiny surface.

5 Leftover fondant can be stored in a
bowl wrapped with cling-film. Before
using again, pour hot water over the
top to soften the hardened top and
let soak for 15 minutes, pour off the
water and heat as usual.

TIPS: Start by mixing lighter fondant
shades first and then add more
fondant and colour as required.
An economic trick is to mix different
coloured icings to achieve a new
colour. Say, to make yellow, blue and
green icing, start with yellow in one
bowl and blue in another. Then mix
these together to make green icing.

Royal Icing and Piping

Piping with royal icing is probably the most essential skill needed for most of my designs, particularly for decorating cookies. Made from icing sugar and either fresh egg white or dried powdered egg white, it also makes an excellent glue for fixing sugar flowers and other decorations on to cakes. Making royal icing is a very simple procedure; should you find it daunting, however, you can buy ready-made versions at specialist cake decorating suppliers.

Royal Icing

STIFF-PEAK CONSISTENCY
For sticking together cake tiers or sticking decorations on to icing

SOFT-PEAK CONSISTENCY
For piping lines, dots and borders

RUNNY CONSISTENCY
For filling in the centre of spaces

INGREDIENTS

about 25g Meri-White (dried egg white powder)
    or whites of 4 medium eggs
1 kg icing sugar, sifted
squeeze of lemon juice

EQUIPMENT

sieve
electric mixer with paddle attachment
wooden spoon or rubber spatula
sealable plastic container
J-cloth

1 If using the Meri-White, mix with water and use as per the packet instructions. Ideally, let this rest overnight in the fridge before use.

2 Place the sugar in the bowl of an electric mixer, add three-quarters of the Meri-White mix or the lightly beaten egg whites and the lemon juice. Start mixing on low speed.

3 Once well combined, check the consistency. If the sides of the bowl still look dry and crumbly, add some more Meri-White or egg white until the icing looks almost smooth but not wet.

4 Keep mixing on low speed for about 4-5 minutes, until it has reached stiff-peak consistency.

5 Spoon into a sealable plastic container, cover with a clean damp J-cloth and the lid. Store at room temperature for up to 7 days; if using fresh egg, store in the refrigerator. The egg white can separate from the sugar after a couple of days, which will turn the icing into a dry, dense mixture. In such a case, remix at low speed until smooth and at stiff-peak consistency again. Make sure that no dried icing bits sticking to the sides of your storage container get into the mixing bowl.

ROYAL ICING CONSISTENCIES

Throughout the book, I refer to the three useful consistencies of royal icing (see page 191), which are important in achieving the right results. Simply thin down your basic royal icing recipe with water, a little bit at a time, using a palette knife, until you have reached the right consistency. Always make sure you keep your icing covered with cling film or a damp cloth when not using it, to stop it from drying out.

Making a Paper Piping Bag

1 Take a rectangular piece of grease-proof paper, about 30x45cm, and cut it from one corner to the opposite one with scissors. Try sliding the scissors through the paper rather than cutting as this gives a cleaner cut.

2 Hold one of the resulting triangles with your hand at the middle of the longest side and with your other hand on the point on the opposite side. The longer side of the triangle should be on your left.

5 If the bag still has an open tip at the front, you can close it by wiggling the inner and outer layers of paper back and forth, until the cone forms a sharp point (see 4).

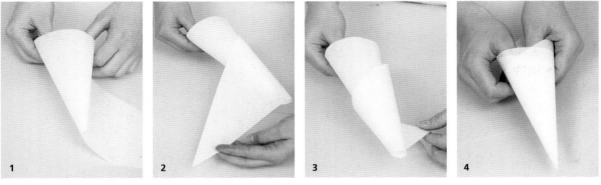

3 Curl the shorter corner on your right over to the corner that is pointing towards you, so that it forms a cone (see 1).

4 With your left hand, wrap the longer corner on the left around the tip of the cone twice and then join it together with the other 2 corners at the back of the cone (see 2 and 3).

6 Fold the corners at the open end into the inside of the bag twice to prevent it unravelling (see 5).

7 Only ever half-fill the bag or icing will ooze out when you squeeze. Close by folding the side with the seam over to the plain side twice.

TIP: For extra strength I use 'waxed' greaseproof paper, also called 'silicon paper', which I buy from a specialist baking supplier.

Piping Techniques

The piping techniques demonstrated below are very useful to practise your general piping skills. Instead of piping directly on to a cake, simply take a piece of greaseproof paper and pipe on to that instead. You can also place templates underneath it and trace them through the paper with your piping bag. If you have never piped with royal icing before, this task is a great way to train your skills, after all practice makes perfect.

First snip a small tip off your piping bag already filled with icing. Hold the bag between the thumb and the fingers of your preferred hand and use the index finger of your other hand to guide the nozzle.

PIPING LINES:

1 Touch the starting point with the tip of the bag and slowly squeeze out the icing. As you are squeezing, lift the bag slightly and pull the line straight towards you or, for example, along the sides of a cookie.

2 Once you are approaching the finishing point, gradually bring the bag down, stop squeezing and drop the line by touching the finishing point with the tip of the bag.

PIPING DOTS:

1 Hold the tip of your piping bag 1mm above the surface and squeeze out the icing to produce a dot on the surface.

2 Gradually lift the tip as the dot gets larger.

3 Once the dot has reached its desired size, stop squeezing and lift off the tip.

4 Should the dot form a little peak at the top, flatten it carefully with a damp soft artist's brush.

PIPING LOOPS AND SWAGS:

1 Start as you would for piping lines.

2 Holding your bag at an angle of 45° to the surface, touch the starting point with the tip and slowly squeeze out the icing. As you squeeze, lift the bag up by about an inch and pull it from one side to the other in circular movements, overlapping the lines in even intervals to create evenly spaced loops and swags.

TIP: If you find it difficult to space the loops and swags out evenly, mark the points where the loops will meet and use them as guides.

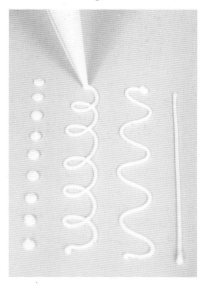

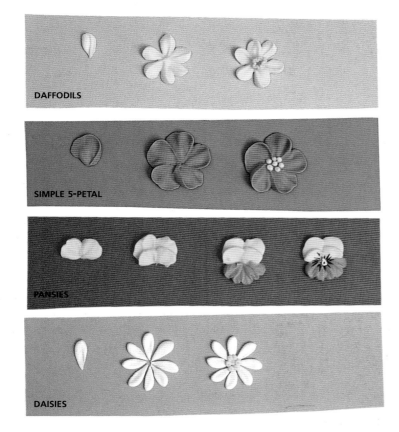

DAFFODILS

SIMPLE 5-PETAL

PANSIES

DAISIES

Royal Iced Flowers

Remember that for the piping of almost all flower shapes, you will want to use icing with a stiff-peak consistency.

EQUIPMENT
metal piping nozzles for petal piping (e.g. Wilton 104, PME 56R, 57R, 58R)

greaseproof paper
scissors
flower nail
paper piping bags (see page 193)
food colours of choice
edible ink pen (black)

PIPING SIMPLE 5-PETAL FLOWERS:

1 From a sheet of greaseproof paper, cut small squares slightly larger than the flower to be piped.

2 Make a paper piping bag and snip the tip off the empty bag to produce an opening large enough to fit a metal piping tube. Drop a Wilton 104 or PME 58R piping nozzle inside the bag, narrow end first.

3 Fill the bag with appropriately coloured stiff-peak icing.

4 Pipe a small dot of icing on top of the flower nail, stick one of the paper squares on top and hold the nail in one hand.

5 Hold the bag in the other hand at a 45 degree angle to the nail, with the wide end touching the centre of the flower nail and the narrow end pointing out and slightly raised.

6 Squeeze out the first petal and give the nail a one-fifth turn as you move the nozzle out towards the edge of the flower nail. Use less pressure as you are moving back towards the centre and curve the nozzle slightly to give the petal a natural shape. Stop squeezing as the wide end touches the centre of the nail and lift up the nozzle.

7 Repeat this 4 more times to make all the petals.

8 Remove the flower with its base paper from the nail and leave to dry.

9 Pipe small yellow dots into the centres as stamens.

NOTE: for smaller flowers, simply use one of the smaller piping tubes listed.

PIPING DAISIES:

1 Use a Wilton 104 piping tube and some stiff-peak white royal icing.

2 Prepare your piping bag and paper squares for the flower nail as above.

3 Mark the centre of the paper-lined nail with a dot of icing.

4 Start at the outer edge of the nail, holding the wide end away from the centre and the narrow end towards the centre of nail.

5 Slightly touch the paper with the wide end of the piping nozzle, squeeze out the icing and pull the nozzle towards the middle as you release the pressure. Stop and pull the tip away.

6 Repeat for 8 or more petals, while turning nail appropriately (see left).

7 Remove the flower with the base paper from the nail and leave to dry.

8 Pipe small yellow dots into the centres as stamens.

NOTE: for smaller flowers, simply use one of the smaller piping tubes.

PIPING PANSIES:

1 You will need 2 piping bags with 2 piping tubes of the same size, one filled with yellow and one filled with purple stiff-peak icing.

2 Start with the yellow icing. Pipe 2 petals next to each other following the same piping technique as for the simple 5-petal flower above.

3 Repeat and pipe 2 shorter yellow petals on top of the larger ones.

4 For the large base petal, tuck the nozzle with the purple icing under the right side of the large yellow petal and start squeezing out a petal the same width as the larger petals, using a back-and-forth hand motion for a ruffled effect.

5 Remove the flower with the paper from the nail and leave to dry.

6 Using a pen filled with edible black ink, draw fine lines into the centre of the pansy.

7 Pipe a fine yellow loop in the middle as a stamen.

PIPING DAFFODILS:

1 Using a PME 58R piping nozzle and egg-yellow stiff-peak icing, pipe a 6-petal flower on top of a paper-lined flower nail, using the same technique as for the daisy.

2 Remove the flower with the base paper from the nail and leave to dry.

3 Pipe 3 rings of pale orange icing on top of each other into the centre of the flower and let the icing dry.

4 Once dry, pipe a fine ruffled line over the edge of the circle.

Making Sugar Roses

Making roses from sugar flower paste is a traditional craft that has always fascinated me. It takes time and skill making this type of rose, as each petal is shaped and stuck on individually, but I find the result very rewarding, as its fine delicate petals look almost natural, which makes it an ideal decoration for a sophisticated wedding cake. The exact amount of sugar flower paste required does, of course, depend on the size of the roses you make.

FOR ABOUT 5 MEDIUM-SIZED ROSES
250g sugar flower paste
small amount of white vegetable fat
selection of edible paste colours
cornflour for dusting
edible glue
selection of blossom tint dusting
   colours

EQUIPMENT
rose petal cutter set (Orchard R1–4)
calyx cutters in different sizes
rose leaf cutters in different sizes
rose leaf veining mat
bone tool
small non-stick plastic board
stay fresh multi mat
small rolling pin
flower foam pad
about 10 teaspoons and 10
   tablespoons
wooden toothpicks
block of Polystyrene or cake dummy
selection of small artist's brushes
small saucepan
sealable plastic bags or cling film

For a rosebud you need 1 centre cone and 3 petals (see page 198, 1–3)

For a half-open rose you need 1 centre cone and 6 petals (page 198, see 4)

For an open rose you need 1 centre cone and 11 petals (page 198, see 5)

For a wide-open rose you need 1 centre cone and 18 petals (page 198, see 6)

The size of roses you need depends on the size of cake they will be used for.

For my Rosy Posy on page 162 and Homage to Cath Kidston cake on page 156, I used cutters R1 (about 4.5cm long) and R2 (about 3.5cm long), but if you have a different rose cutter set it will do just as well.

Make the rose centres at least a day ahead.

1 Knead the flower paste until smooth and pliable and add a small amount of the white vegetable fat if it feels hard and brittle.

2 Knead in the paste colour as required, a little at the time. If you want to make different colours of roses, divide the paste into portions and dye them first. Wrap in a sealable plastic bag and rest for about 30 minutes. Allow some extra for the green leaves.

3 To shape the rose centres take a small piece of flower paste and shape it to a cone that is slightly shorter than the petal cutter.

4 Apply a thin layer of vegetable fat to one end of a toothpick with your fingers. Then push the greased end vertically into the bottom of the cone. Stick the toothpick into the styrofoam or cake dummy and let the cone dry for a couple of hours, ideally overnight. Prepare all the cones you need.

TO MAKE THE ROSEBUDS

5 To make the rose petals, place a piece of sugar flower paste on the plastic board dusted lightly with cornflour. Roll out until very thin, about 1mm. Stamp out petal shapes making sure edges are clean and sharp. Remove excess paste around the petals and wrap for later use. Cover the petals with the multi mat to stop them drying out

6 Place petal no. 1 on the foam pad. Keep the remaining petals covered.

7 Shape and stretch it by gently running the bone tool from the centre to the outside edge. Notice how the petal becomes slightly larger and the edge begins to frill.

8 Brush the surface of the petal thinly with edible glue, using a fine artist's brush.

9 Wrap tightly around the cone, round side up, making sure the tip is completely covered.

10 For the second row of rose petals, take another 2 petals from the plastic board and repeat steps 8 & 9.

11 Brush the bottom half of both petals thinly with the edible glue. Position the first of the 2 petals centred over the seam. Tuck the other slightly inside the previous petal and push the sides together. Slightly curve the edges out with your fingertips.

TO MAKE A HALF-OPEN ROSE:

12 Continue by laying another 3 petals the same size around the rosebud, each slightly overlapping. Again slightly curve the edges of the petals out with your fingertips.

TO MAKE AN OPEN ROSE

13 Before continuing with the next layer of petals make sure that the half-open rose is completely dry.

14 Shape another 5 petals that are a size larger than the previous one, as described in step 7, and lay each inside a spoon dusted with cornflower with the edges slightly overlapping the spoon. Curve the edges of the petals to the outside with your fingertips and them it dry for about 15 minutes, until they feel slightly rubbery. Letting the petals semi-dry inside a spoon gives them more volume and shape and they will look more realistic.

15 Brush the bottom half of both petals thinly with the edible glue and arrange them around the half-open rose as before. You may find that the petals are now a little bit too heavy to hold up while still wet. In this case turn the rose carefully upside down on to the polystyrene block or cake dummy and let dry.

TO MAKE A LARGE OPEN ROSE
16 Repeat steps 13 to 15 using 7 petals.

DUSTING AND STEAMING SUGAR ROSES
17 Once all roses have completely dried, you can enhance and highlight their colour by dusting the edges of the petals with blossom tint colours of a complementary shade. For example, I have used plum for dusting the purple and pink roses on my Rosy Posy on page 162.

18 Dip a fine artist's brush into a small amount of colour powder and brush the edges of the petals with it from the outside towards the centre. You have to be very careful not to spill any colour as it is almost impossible to take it off. Shake off any excess powder.

19 Once you have dusted all your roses, boil some water in a small pan and hold each rose carefully over the steam for about 3 seconds. This will bring the colour to life and give the rose a satin-like sheen.

TO MAKE CALYXES AND LEAVES
20 Roll out some green flower paste to about 1mm thickness and stamp out the calyx and leaf shapes. Remove the excess paste and keep it covered for later use.

21 Place the calyx on to the foam pad and gently move the bone tool over its surface from the centre towards the edges to stretch and thin the edges slightly. Keep the leaves covered until later.

22 Brush a thin layer of edible glue over the top and stick it underneath the bottom of the rose. Pinch and shape the tips with your fingers as required.

23 Place the leaves on the foam pad and again gently stretch and thin the edges with the bone tool.

24 Press each leaf in the rose leaf veiner and shape slightly with your fingers for a natural look.

TIPS:
Hand-crafted sugar roses can be made weeks or even months in advance as they have a very long shelf-life. Make sure you protect them from dust and sunlight to keep the colour.

• Use a lighter colour shade for the centre of the rose and a darker one for the outside petals or vice versa. This will make your rose look even more natural.

• Some blossom tints are not edible, so check the label and remove the flowers from the cake before eating if you use those colours.

Glossary

Most items are available from specialist suppliers (opposite), although more everyday ones can be found in supermarkets and cookware shops.

INGREDIENTS

FONDANT Made from sugar, water and cream of tartar, fondant is widely used as a glaze in confectionery as well as in pâtisserie and cake decorating. Ready-made fondant is available in a block or as a powder to be mixed with water.

GLUCOSE, LIQUID A thick version of corn syrup used to make fondant icing in order to give a beautiful shine.

GUM TRAGACANTH Made from the dried sap of the Astragalus plant, this is sold as a powdered hardening agent and is mixed with sugar paste to create a pliable modelling paste for making sugar flowers. It has the further effect of making the paste set on contact with air. It may also be mixed with a little water to make an edible glue.

LUSTRE (OR LUSTER), EDIBLE This non-toxic pearl dust comes in different shades. It can either be mixed to a thick paste with a drop of alcohol or applied directly with an artist's brush.

MARZIPAN Made from ground almonds and icing sugar, marzipan is used for covering large cakes before icing, as it seals in moisture as well as helping to stabilise shape. It is also ideal for making flowers, as it is very easy to mould and the individual petals stick to each other naturally.

MERI-WHITE This is dried egg white powder used instead of fresh egg whites in making royal icing for food safety reasons, as the dried egg white is pasteurized.

SUGAR FLORIST PASTE OR GUM PASTE A fine and pliable paste made from icing sugar, gelatine and gum tragacanth, which dries hard, with a porcelain-like texture. It is used to make finely crafted sugar flowers.

SUGAR PASTE A very smooth and pliable icing made from gelatine, icing sugar and water, which dries hard but is still easy to cut. Sugar paste is used for covering cakes and for making flowers and modelling cake decorations.

EQUIPMENT

BONE TOOL A long plastic stick with rounded ends, looking like a bone, this is used to shape sugar paste petals.

CAKE SMOOTHERS These are flat rectangular pieces of smooth plastic, with a handle, used to smooth the marzipan and sugar paste on a cake.

DESIGN WHEELER A plastic sugar craft tool with 3 interchangeable heads for creating patterns and designs, such as stitching, on sugar paste cakes.

DRESDEN TOOL A tool for fluting petals. Its pointed tip is used to emphasize flower centres, the other to make vein markings.

FLOWER CUTTERS Made of metal or plastic, flower cutters are used to cut petals and leaves out of flower paste. In this book I have used cutters to make violets, stephanotis, petunias and primroses.

FLOWER FOAM PAD This is used as a yielding surface for thinning the edges of flower paste with a bone tool (above).

FLOWER STAMEN Similar to the stamen used for silk flowers, these contain small wires and are used for sugar flower centres, although they are NOT edible.

LINEN-LOOK ROLLING PIN A plastic rolling pin with a textured surface that embosses a linen effect into icing.

MARZIPAN SPACERS Long sticks used to roll out dough, sugar paste or marzipan to an even thickness.

PETAL/LEAF VEINING MAT Rubber mat for shaping and marking leaves and petals.

PROFILE FOAM SHEET A sheet of textured packaging foam with wells (similar to a egg box); useful to support the shape of sugar flowers and leaves when drying.

SCRIBER NEEDLE A fine metal pin used to mark/scratch patterns into icing.

SIDE SCRAPER Flat piece of metal (ideally stainless steel) with a straight side used for scraping excess cream off the side of a cake when filling. It helps give perfectly straight sides.

SIDE SCRIBING/MARKING GAUGE A height-adjustable tool to scribe markings into icing in straight lines.

STAY FRESH MULTI MAT Thick acetate mat used to cover rolled-out sugar (flower) paste to prevent drying out.

Suppliers

FOR CAKE DECORATING TOOLS, FOOD COLOURS AND EQUIPMENT:

UK
Jane Asher Party Cakes
24 Cale Street
London SW3 3QU
www.jane-asher.co.uk

Almond Art
Unit 15/16
Faraday Close
Gorse Lane Industrial Estate
Clacton-on-Sea, Essex
CO15 4TR
tel 01255 223322
www.almondart.com

Squires Shop and School
Squires House
3 Waverley Lane
Farnham, Surrey
GU9 8BB
www.squires-group.co.uk

FOR FLOWER CUTTERS, VEINERS AND CAMEO MOULDS:
Design A Cake
30–31 Phoenix Road
Crowther Industrial Estate
Washington
Tyne & Wear
NE38 0AD
www.design-a-cake.co.uk

ASIA
International Centre of Cake Artistry
Sdn. Bhd.
1-1 to 1-3A, Jalan PJU 5/15
Dataran Sunway
Kota Damansara
47810 Petaling Jaya,
Selangor, Malaysia
tel 603 6140 8835
www.2decoratecakes.com

AUSTRALIA & NEW ZEALAND
Cake Deco
Shop 7, Port Phillip Arcade
232 Flinders Street, Melbourne,
Victoria
Australia
www.cakedeco.com.au

Milly's
273 Ponsonby Road
Auckland, New Zealand
tel 09 376 1550
www.millyskitchen.co.nz

GERMANY
Tortissimo Backzubehör
Carl-Benz-Str. 6
35305 Grünberg, Deutschland
www.tortissimo.de

THE NETHERLANDS
De Leukste Taarten Shop
Meeuwstraat 10
1546 LR Jisp, Holland
www.deleukstetaartenshop.nl

USA & CANADA
Global Sugar Art
28 Plattsburgh Plaza
Plattsburgh, NY 12901
tel 518 561 3039
www.globalsugarart.com

Creative Cutters
561 Edward Avenue, Unit 2
Richmond Hill, Ontario
Canada L4C 9W6
www.creativecutters.com

Quantity Guides

CAKE MIX QUANTITY AND PORTION GUIDE

This chart will give an overview of what size cake you need for your number of guests and the approximate quantity of cake mix needed for the different sizes of cake tins.

The basic cake recipes in this book are based on a 20cm cake tin or 20–24 cup cakes or 25 fondant fancies. Please bear in mind that for each cake tier you will need 2 sponges, i.e. double the amount of cake mix, baked in 2 tins of the same size. The figure shown in the second column below indicates by how much the basic recipe needs to be multiplied.

CAKE TIN SIZE (ROUND OR SQUARE)	MULTIPLY BASIC RECIPE BY	CAKE PORTIONS 2.5X2.5CM (1X1 INCH) ROUND/SQUARE	MINI CAKES	CUP CAKES	FONDANT FANCIES
10cm (4 inch)	¼	10 / 16			
12.5cm (5 inch)	⅓	12 / 20			
15cm (6 inch)	½	20 / 35			
17.5cm (7 inch)	¾	25 / 45			
20cm (8 inch)	1	40 / 60	9	20-24	25
22.5cm (9 inch)	1⅓	50 / 80			
25cm (10 inch)	2	60 / 100	16	40-48	36
27.5cm (11 inch)	2½	80 / 120			
30cm (12 inch)	3¼	90 / 140	25		
35cm (14 inch)	4¼	130 / 185			

QUANTITY GUIDE FOR MARZIPAN AND SUGAR PASTE, AND BUTTERCREAM OR CHOCOLATE GANACHE FILLING

The figures below give you the approximate amounts required for cakes of different sizes, round or square, with a height of 8.5cm (3½ inches).

CAKE / BOARD SIZE	MARZIPAN / SUGAR PASTE	SUGAR PASTE FOR CAKE BOARD	BUTTERCREAM / GANACHE
10cm (4 inch)	400g		150g (also 25 fondant fancies)
12.5cm (5 inch)	500g		225g
15cm (6 inch)	600g	300g	300g
17.5cm (7 inch)	750g	400g	450g (also 20–24 cup cakes)
20cm (8 inch)	850g	600g	600g
22.5cm (9 inch)	1kg	700g	750g
25cm (10 inch)	1.25kg	800g	900g
27.5cm (11 inch)	1.5kg	850g	1.2kg
30cm (12 inch)	1.75kg	900g	1.5kg
32.5cm (13 inch)	2kg	950g	1.75kg
35cm (14 inch)	2.5kg	1kg	2kg

Index

Templates

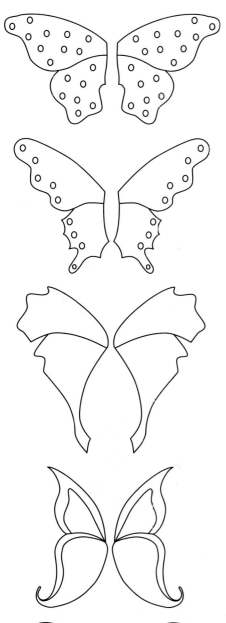

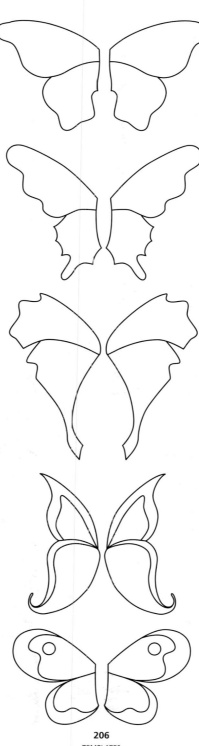

This basic butterfly template can be reduced or enlarged as required to make butterflies of the appropriate sizes.

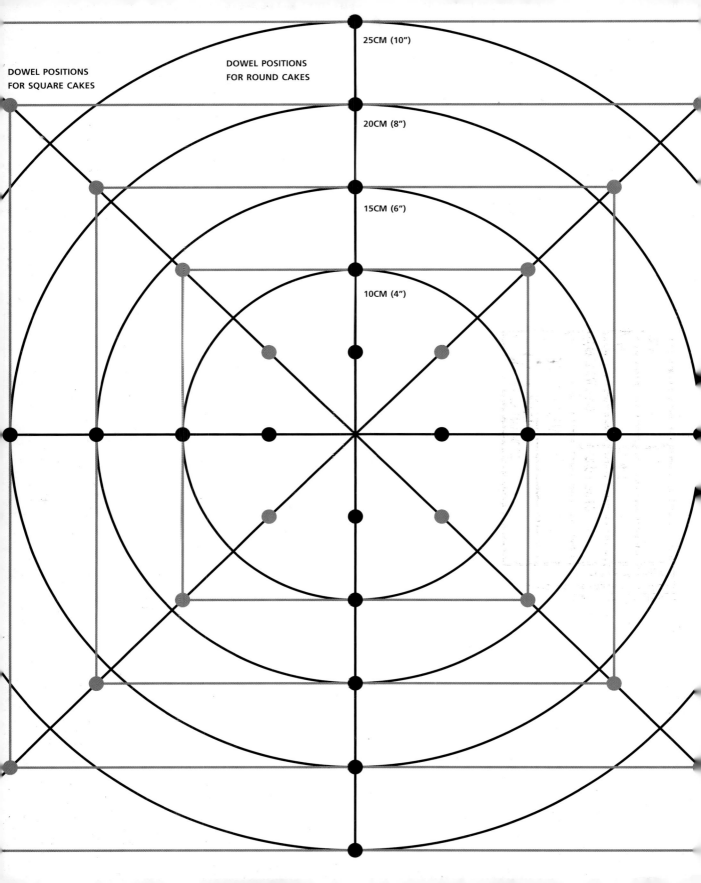

DOWEL POSITIONS FOR SQUARE CAKES

DOWEL POSITIONS FOR ROUND CAKES

25CM (10")

20CM (8")

15CM (6")

10CM (4")